Resonation Techniques

Resonation amplifies the sound that is produced through the vocal folds. Think of the holes in the bone structure of your face as a speaker. Resonation techniques help you to use that speaker more effectively as a singer and it will improve the tone quality and general sound of your voice when you sing and speak.

Here are some exercises for you to use that will assist you in finding out where your voice resonates the best. Use these techniques as you speak throughout the day to lessen the stress that is placed on the vocal folds when you talk.

1. Begin by placing your fingers over your mouth, cheeks and nose.
2. Say mmm-hmmm several times with your mouth closed and your jaw open. You have found your best resonation when you fell a significant vibration in the mask of your face.
3. Now say mmm hmmm and allide these vowels with it

A as in mate	mmm hmm a
E as in me	mmm hmm e
Ah as in saw	mmm hmm ah
O as in hope	mmm hmm o
Oo as in move	mmm hmm oo

4. Do this exercise at least 10 times in a row while you continue to use your breathing techniques. As you improve with your breathing and resonation I will add to this exercise. This will help you solidify your resonance and make it easier for you to sing later on.

Resonation Techniques

Resonation amplifies the sound that is produced through the vocal folds. Think of the holes in the bone structure of your face as a speaker. Resonation techniques help you to use that speaker more effectively as a singer and it will improve the tone quality and general sound of your voice when you sing and speak.

Here are some exercises for you to use that will assist you in finding out where your voice resonates the best. Use these techniques as you speak throughout the day to lessen the stress that is placed on the vocal folds when you talk.

1. Begin by placing your fingers over your mouth, cheeks and nose.
2. Say mmm-hmmm several times with your mouth closed and your jaw open. You have found your best resonation when you fell a significant vibration in the mask of your face.
3. Now say mmm hmmm and allide these vowels with it

A as in mate	mmm hmm a
E as in me	mmm hmm e
Ah as in saw	mmm hmm ah
O as in hope	mmm hmm o
Oo as in move	mmm hmm oo

4. Do this exercise at least 10 times in a row while you continue to use your breathing techniques. As you improve with your breathing and resonation I will add to this exercise. This will help you solidify your resonance and make it easier for you to sing later on.

BASIC THEORY—HARMONY

A TEXT AND WORK BOOK
for the
SCHOOL MUSICIAN

by

Joseph Paulson

and

Irving Cheyette

Foreword

THEORY and HARMONY should be studied by all music students in order that they may further the development of their musicianship, whether they are singers, pianists or instrumentalists. Such a course will acquaint them with the structure and form of the art they perform.

Although this book is written along modern lines, it has included Figured Bass since such study is still required in many colleges. However, modern chord names and symbols are introduced, and the reason for the change from the traditional system is clearly explained.

For the past generation, theorists have been gradually changing or eliminating old rules of harmony. This has been a slow process, since each one has been reluctant to face the criticism of the conformists.

Just as everything else has changed since the days of Bach and Handel, so has music changed. Modern music is with us, so we might as well try to understand it and to study along modern lines. Except for certain fundamental principles which will always remain, there can be no hard and fast rules. The theory of today was not used a hundred years ago, and may not be good in another hundred years.

This book is intended to cover two years of class study. While the use of a piano is recommended, much of the work should be done through singing of exercises in order to develop the ear. Student studies should be played through at the piano, so that they may hear harmonically what they have written. Chapter 8 on Ear Training should be referred to frequently.

The book is organized into a combination of text and work book containing all the exercises in one volume. This means that the student will have a permanent reference available to him as he prepares his studies, and will be able to keep all of his work in the one volume. It will also save the instructor much valuable time in making assignments since they are all prepared for the student in the book. Any additional studies prepared on manuscript paper may then be inserted into the book at the proper lesson page.

We feel that completion of such a course will give the school music student keener insight and a finer appreciation into the great art of music.

Contents

CHAPTER I
Clefs and Notation

A Clef is a character used to determine the name and pitch of the notes on the staff to which it is prefixed. There are four clefs in common use today.

The Soprano or Treble clef fixes G on the second line. The Bass clef fixes F on the fourth line. The Alto clef fixes middle C on the third line. The Tenor clef fixes middle C on the fourth line. The object of the last two clefs is to avoid use of leger lines. Leger lines are light lines added above or below the staff to extend the pitch range of the staff. In the study of harmony, it is necessary to know the first two clefs. Band and orchestra students are usually only familiar with one.

STUDY THE FOLLOWING CHART

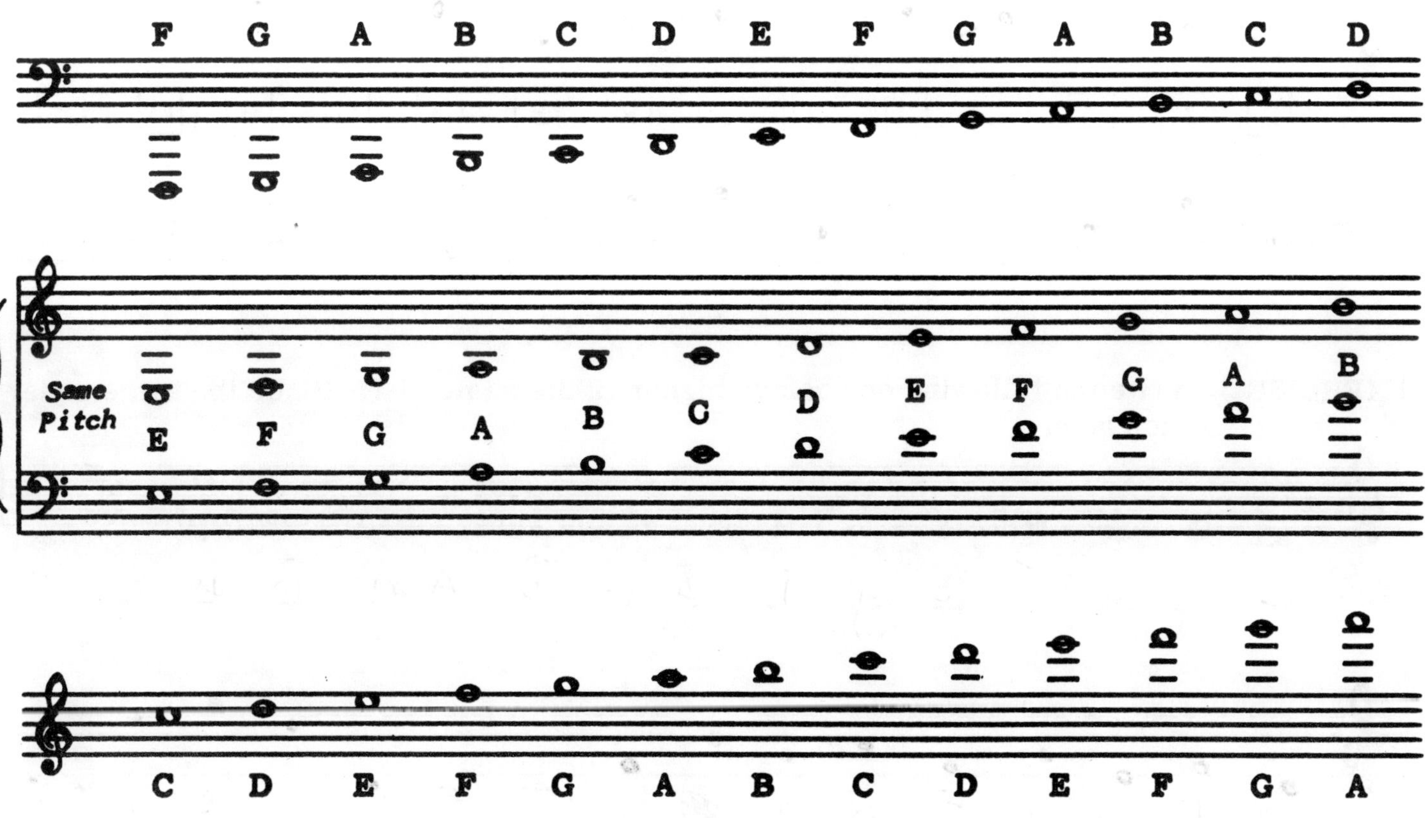

EXERCISE 1. Place the name under each of the following notes.

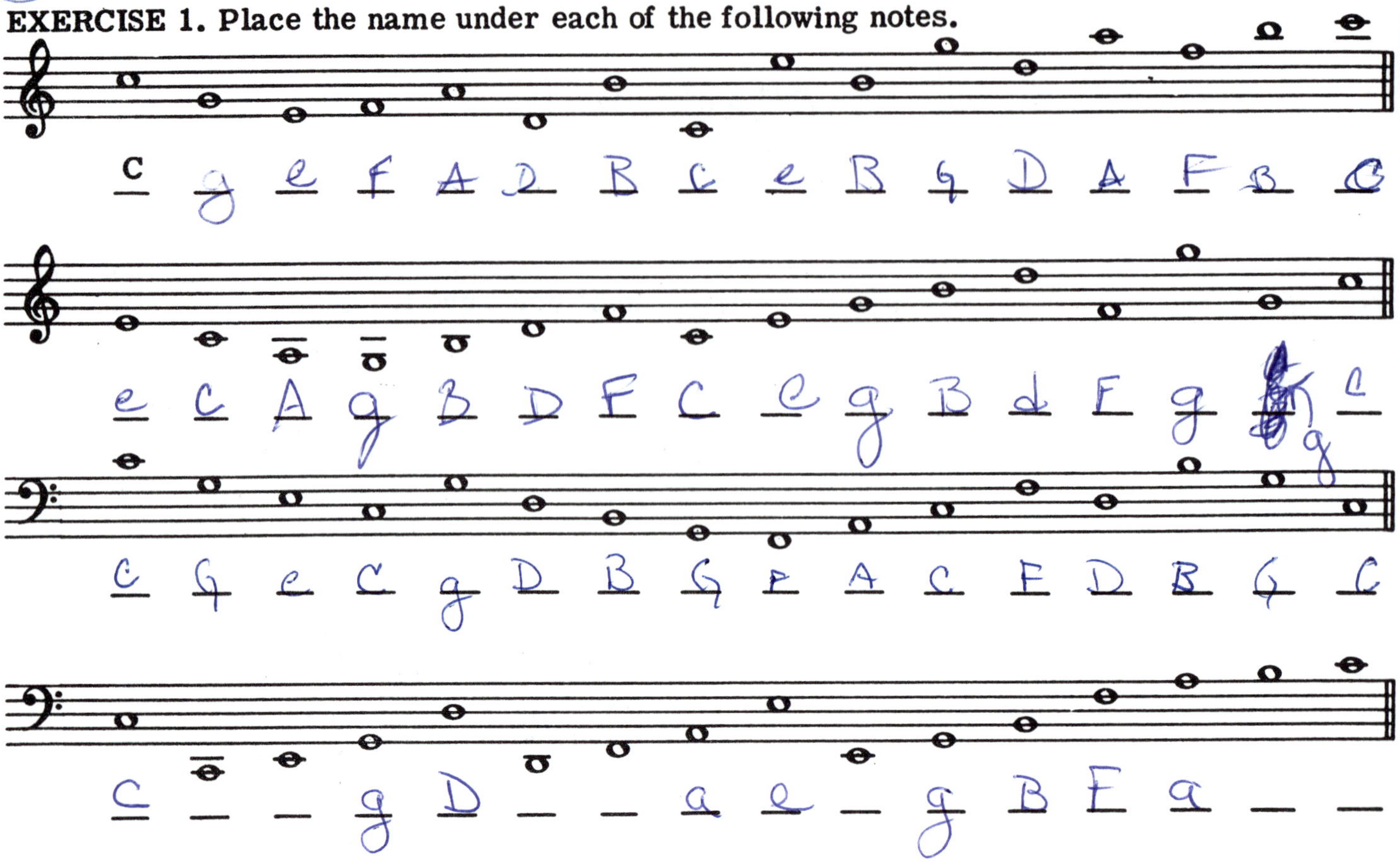

C

EXERCISE 2. Write the following within the staff in both clefs.

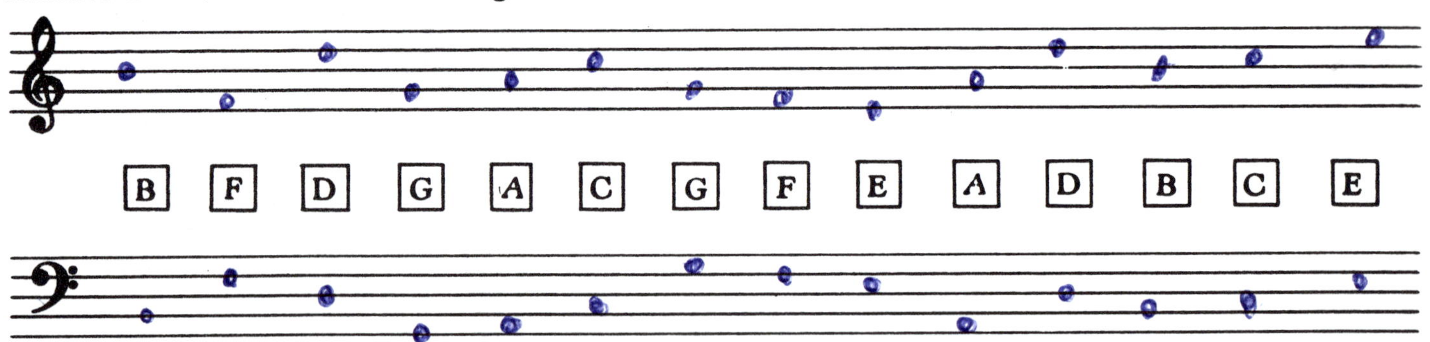

EXERCISE 3. Write the following one octave higher in the same clef. Place the name under each note.

EXERCISE 4. Write the following treble clef notes in the bass, one octave below. Place the name under each note.

EXERCISE 5. Write the following bass clef notes in the treble, one octave above. Place the name under each note.

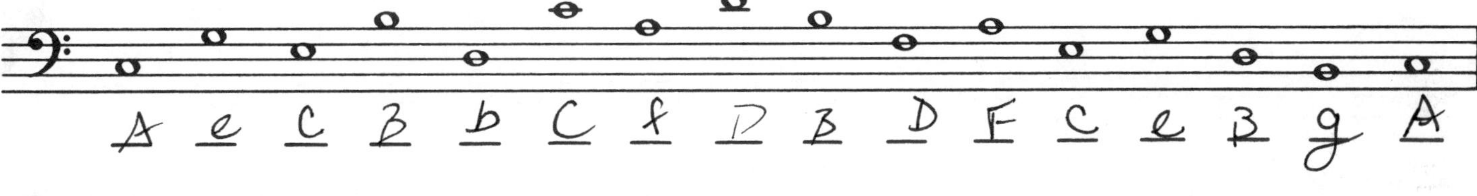

EXERCISE 6. Write the following treble clef notes in the bass, in the same pitch. Place the name under each note.

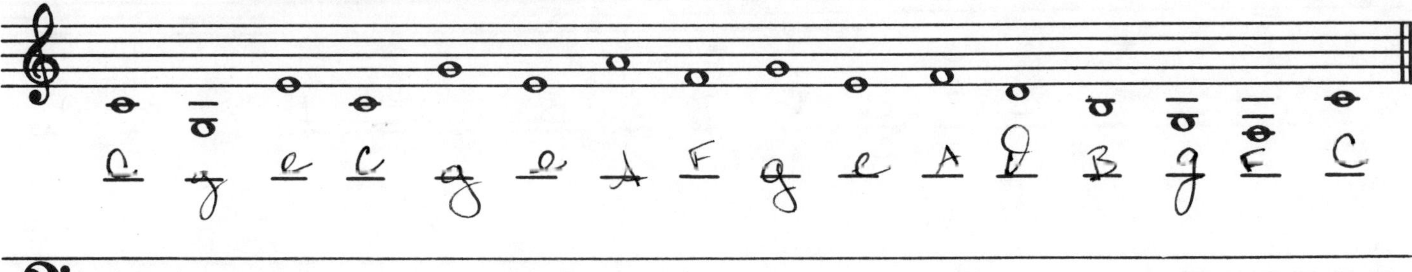

EXERCISE 7. Write the following bass clef notes in the treble, in the same pitch. Place the name under each note.

EXERCISE 8. Write the following treble clef notes in the bass, two octaves below. Place the name under each note.

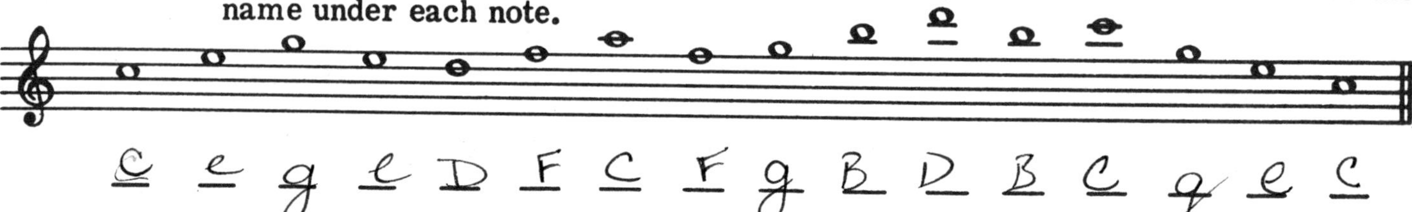

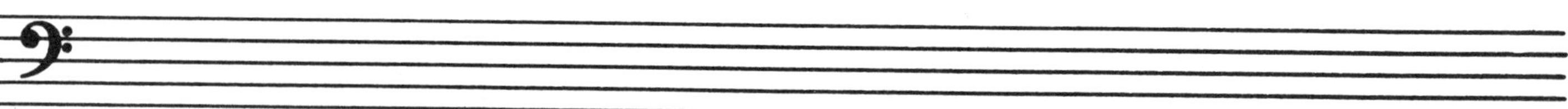

EXERCISE 9. Write the following bass clef notes in the treble, two octaves above. Place the name under each note.

CHAPTER 2
Major Scales and Signatures

Each line and space, on, above and below the staff is called a degree. A Diatonic Major scale is composed of eight tones within the octave, with half steps between the third and fourth, and seventh and eighth degrees. Degrees are always counted upward from the lowest tone. Each Major scale takes its name from its lowest tone or first degree. The four tones comprising each half of a major scale, are called a Tetrachord.

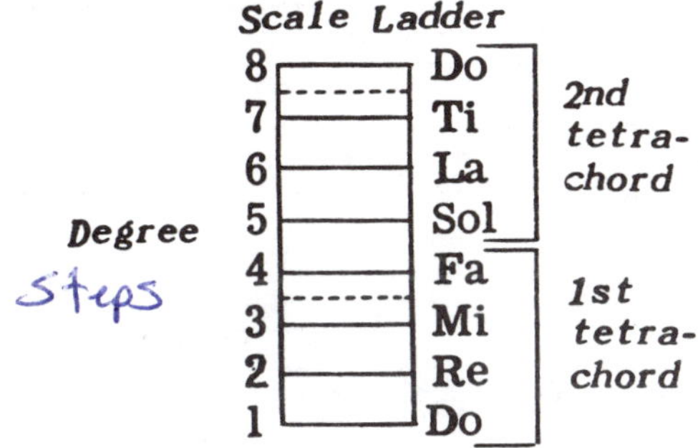

The scale is built from two tetrachords, each of four tones, consisting of whole step, whole step, and half step.

In forming the next scale, the upper half of C major becomes the lower half of G major. A sharp is added to form the half step between the seventh and eighth degrees. The upper tetrachord of C major becomes the first tetrachord of G major.

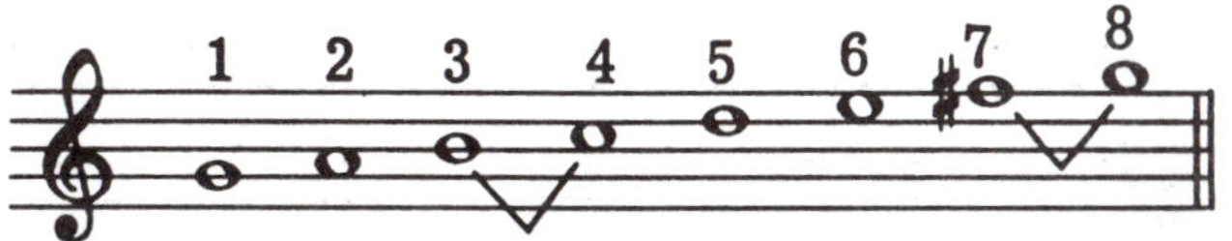

In forming the next scale, the upper half of G major becomes the lower half of D major, and another sharp is added. The upper tetrachord of G major is now the first tetrachord of D major.

Notice that the new sharp is always added to the seventh degree.

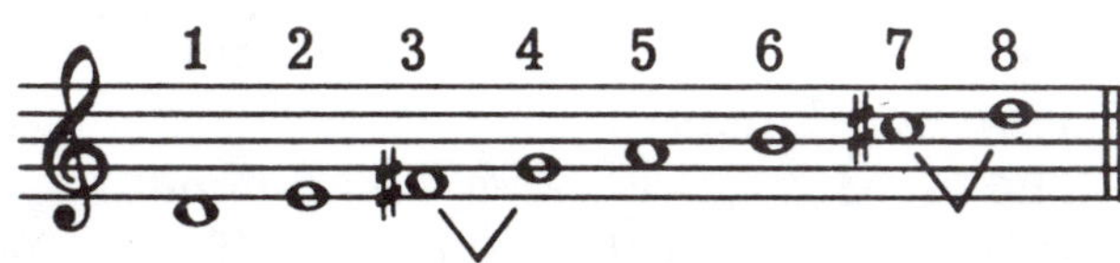

This process continues until each note has had a sharp.

To form the flat scales, this process is reversed. The C major scale is raised an octave for convenience in writing. The eighth degree may also be the first degree of the octave above.

In forming the first flat scale, the lower half of C major descending becomes the upper half of F major. A flat is added to form the half step between the third and fourth degrees. Which tetrachord of C major has now become a tetrachord in F major?

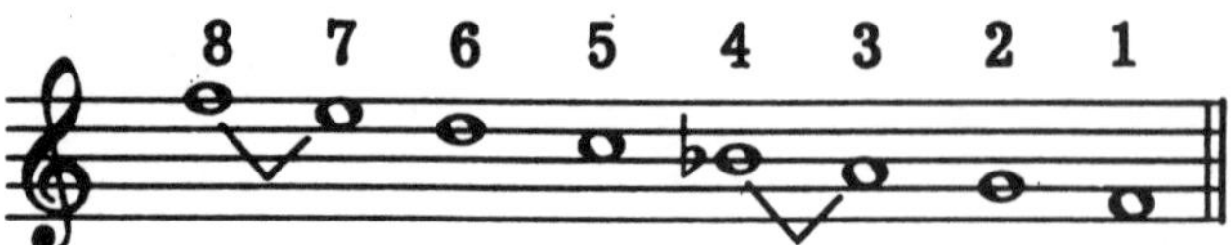

In forming the next scale, the lower half of F major becomes the upper half of B♭ major, and another flat is added. Which tetrachord of F major has become a tetrachord of B♭ major?

Notice that the new flat is always added to the 4th degree.

This process continues until each note has had a flat.

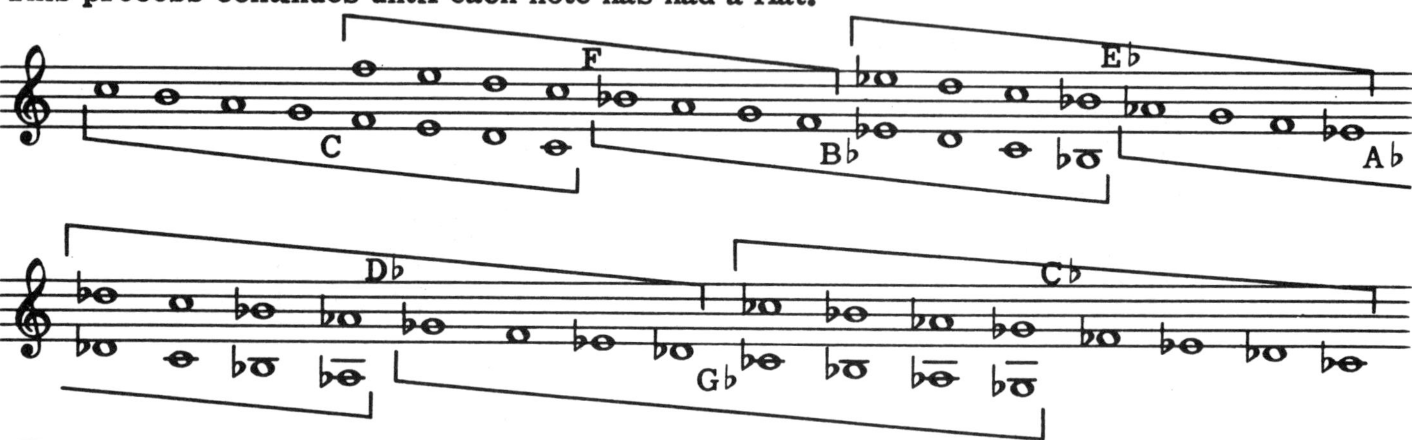

When a note is given a different letter name but retains its same pitch, it is called an enharmonic change.

The scales of F♯ and G♭ are enharmonic, that is, identical in pitch but different notation. The scales of C♯ and C♭ are seldom used. Their enharmonic equivalents, D♭ and B are used instead.

We now show all the major scales ascending in their correct sequence.

Study carefully the overlapping tetrachords of the cycle of keys.

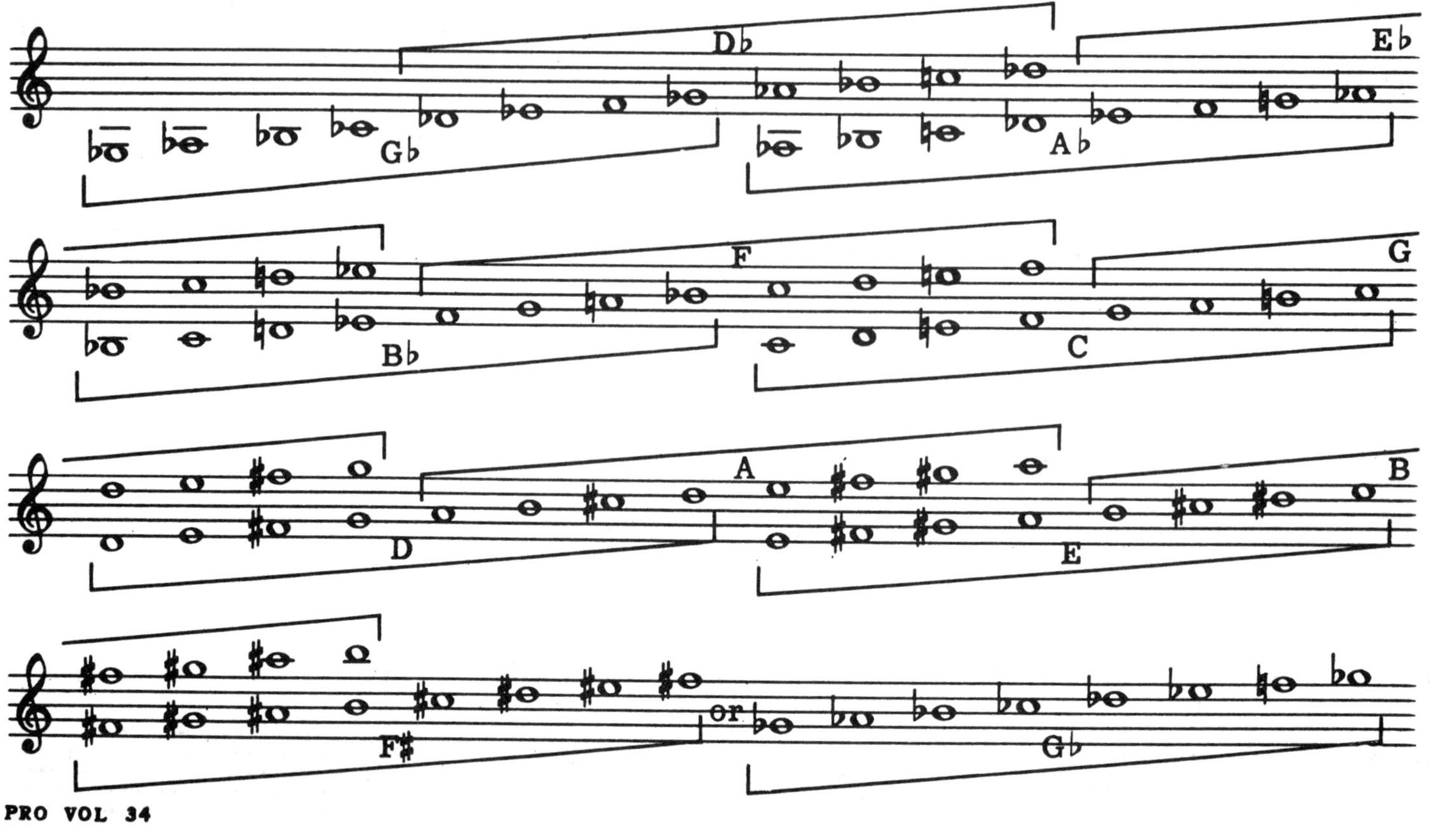

The combination of sharps and flats necessary to form a major scale, is called a key signature. Sharps and flats are written on the staff in this order.

Notice that the order of flats is **opposite to** the order of sharps.

F♯ C♯ G♯ D♯ A♯ E♯ B♯

B♭ E♭ A♭ D♭ G♭ C♭ F♭

TABLE OF KEYS AND SIGNATURES

C MAJOR has no sharps or flats

G MAJOR has one sharp,	F♯
D MAJOR has two sharps,	F♯ C♯
A MAJOR has three sharps,	F♯ C♯ G♯
E MAJOR has four sharps,	F♯ C♯ G♯ D♯
B MAJOR has five sharps,	F♯ C♯ G♯ D♯ A♯
F♯ MAJOR has six sharps,	F♯ C♯ G♯ D♯ A♯ E♯
C♯ MAJOR has seven sharps,	F♯ C♯ G♯ D♯ A♯ E♯ B♯
F MAJOR has one flat,	B♭
B♭ MAJOR has two flats,	B♭ E♭
E♭ MAJOR has three flats,	B♭ E♭ A♭
A♭ MAJOR has four flats,	B♭ E♭ A♭ D♭
D♭ MAJOR has five flats,	B♭ E♭ A♭ D♭ G♭
G♭ MAJOR has six flats,	B♭ E♭ A♭ D♭ G♭ C♭
C♭ MAJOR has seven flats,	B♭ E♭ A♭ D♭ G♭ C♭ F♭

A Cycle in music is a succession of intervals, keys or chords which recur in regular order. The following diagram of the cycle of keys will show the relationship of all the major scales, three of which may be written in either sharp or flat keys.

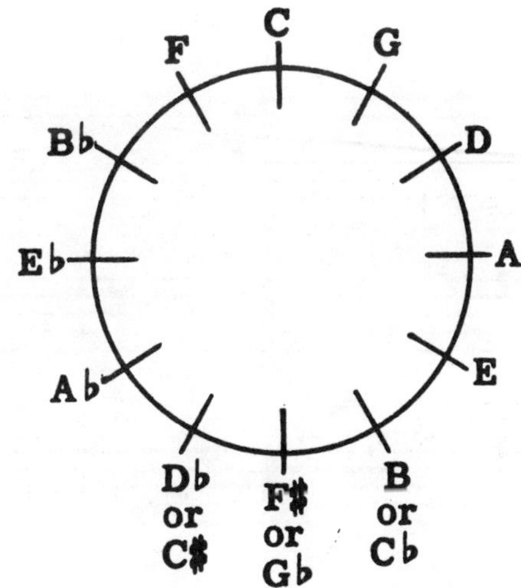

The most important degrees in each key are 1-3-5, which form the Tonic or I chord of the key.

EXERCISE 10. Write the 1-3-5 or Tonic of the following keys: G, F, D, E♭, A.

EXERCISE 11. Fill in the necessary sharps and flats in the following major scales. Write the scale degree under each note. Sing these scales with the pitch names. When they go out of vocal range drop down an octave or up an octave as is necessary.

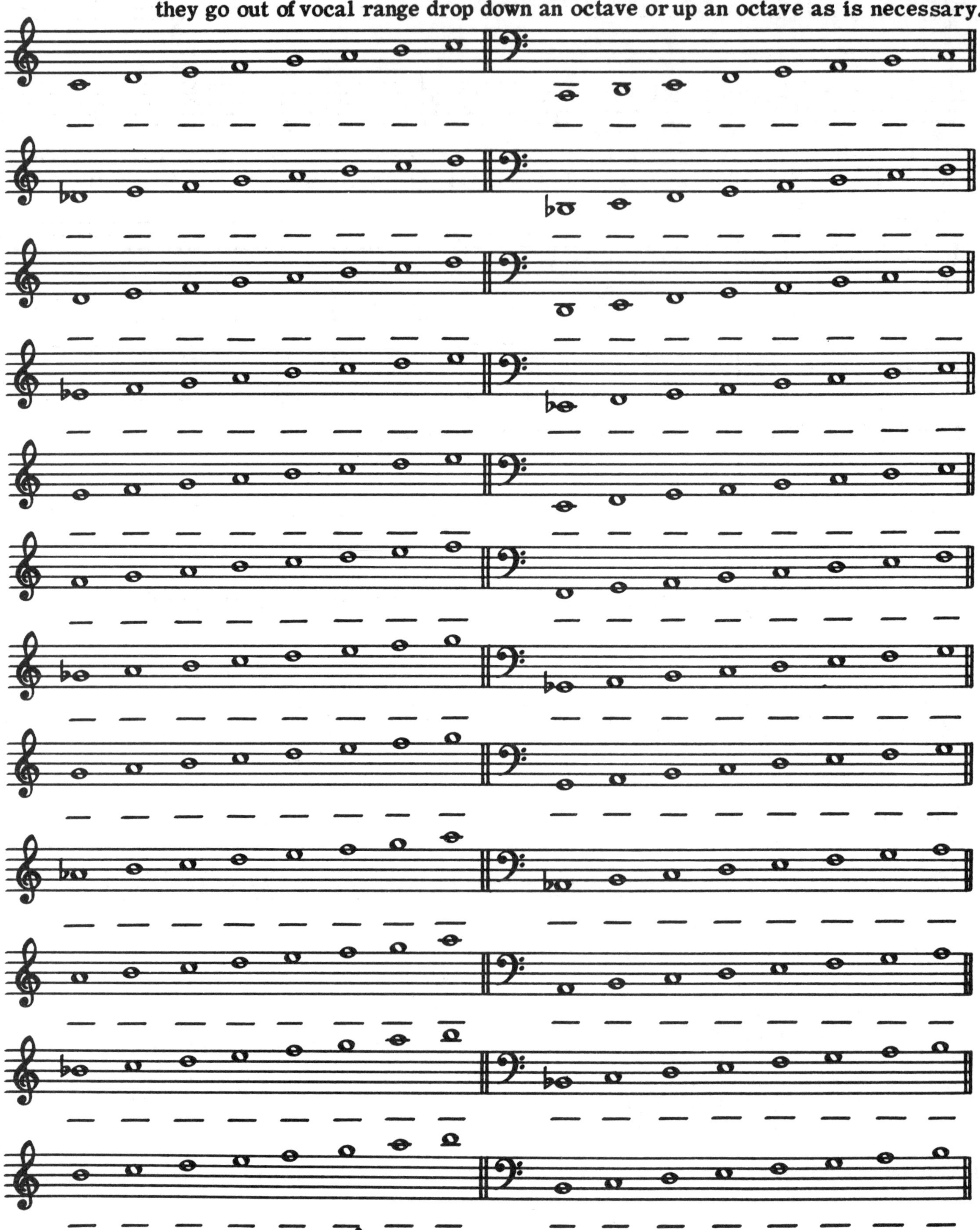

EXERCISE 12. Name the key of the following signatures.

EXERCISE 13. Write the signatures of the following keys in both clefs. D, E♭, G, B♭, A, F, E, A♭, B, D♭.

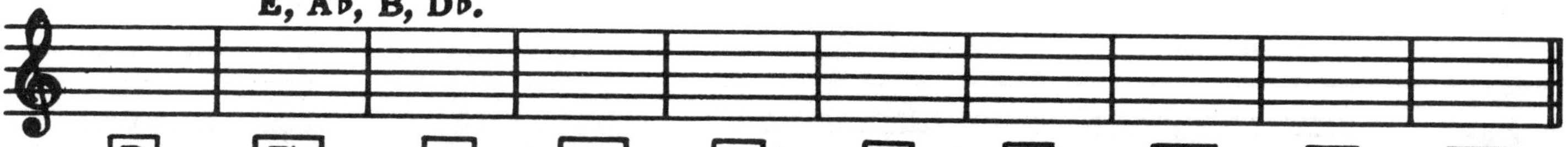

D E♭ G B♭ A F E A♭ B D♭

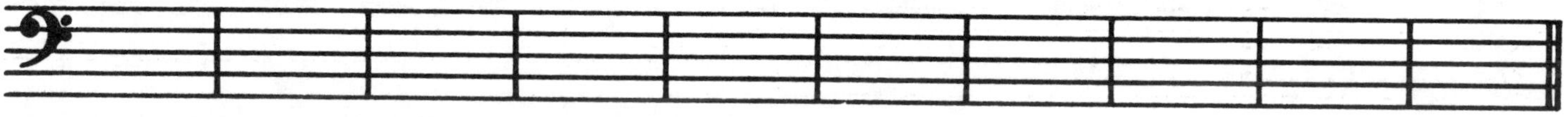

EXERCISE 14. Change the following notes enharmonically.

Example *Double sharp*

EXERCISE 15. Write and name the 7th degree in the scales of: D, A♭, C, E, F, A.

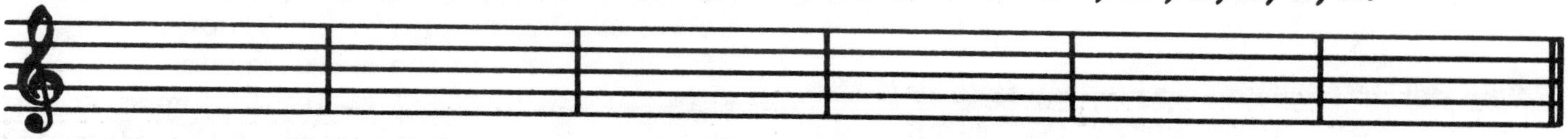

EXERCISE 16. Write and name the 2nd degree in the scales of: B♭, D♭, E♭, G, A♭, F.

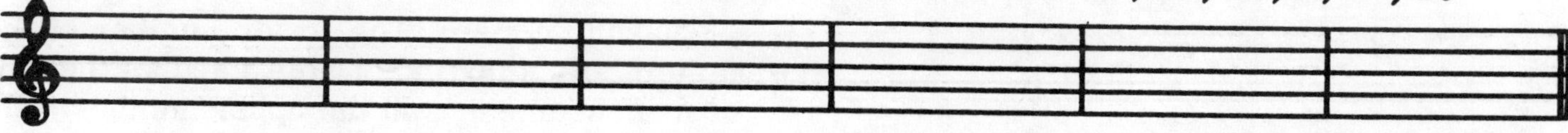

Any note can belong to seven different keys.

C is 1 in the key of C.
C is 2 in the key of B♭.
C is 3 in the key of A♭.
C is 4 in the key of G.
C is 5 in the key of F.
C is 6 in the key of E♭.
C is 7 in the key of D♭.

Sharps and flats are sometimes changed enharmonically when they are put in different keys.

A♭ is 1 in the key of A♭.
A♭ is 2 in the key of G♭.
G♯ (not A♭) is 3 in the key of E.

EXERCISE 17. Write a table like the above, showing the seven keys to which the note G belongs.

CHAPTER 3
Time Values and Meters

Time values are expressed by notes, rests and dots.

RELATIVE NOTE VALUES

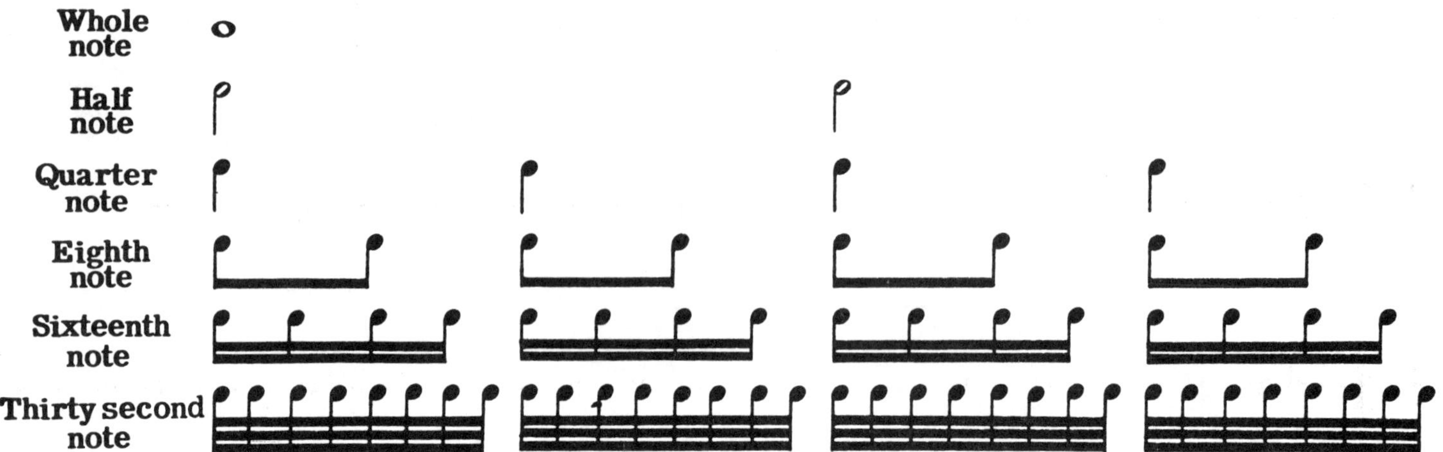

The last three may be written singly instead of in groups.

Eighth Sixteenth Thirty-second

REST VALUES

Whole rest
Half rest
Quarter rest
Eighth rest
Sixteenth rest
Thirty-second rest

The whole rest may also be used as a WHOLE MEASURE rest, and fills a measure of any length, $\frac{3}{4}$ $\frac{6}{8}$ $\frac{12}{8}$ etc.

The dot has a time value equal to half the value of the note or rest after which it is placed.

When the double dot is used, the second dot equals half the value of the first dot. and so on, applied to notes or rests of all denominations.

Rhythm is the motion of music.
Meter is the measurement of this motion.

CLASSIFICATION OF VARIOUS METERS

$\frac{2}{4}$ $\frac{3}{4}$ $\frac{4}{4}$ $\frac{5}{4}$ $\frac{6}{4}$ $\frac{9}{4}$ $\frac{2}{2}$ $\frac{3}{2}$ $\frac{3}{8}$ $\frac{4}{8}$ $\frac{6}{8}$ $\frac{9}{8}$ $\frac{12}{8}$

In the first group, the quarter note is the unit of measurement, in the second group, the half note, and in the third group, the eighth note. Sometimes $\frac{4}{4}$ meter is expressed by the sign C. $\frac{2}{2}$ is expressed by ₵, called Alla Breve or Cut Time.

To summarize: The lower number of the meter tells the kind of note used as the unit of measurement, and the upper number tells how many in a measure.

A measure is one complete round or count of the Meter, containing notes, rests or dots of relative value.

A Bar is a line on the staff separating each measure. The term Bar is sometimes used to mean Measure.

The Beat is the pulse of rhythm, as in the ticking of a clock, or the tread of marching feet. It sometimes occurs on each unit of measurement, and sometimes on the first of every group of two, three or four units.

EXERCISE 18. Complete the time values in each of the following measures, using either notes, rests or dots, according to the space available.

EXERCISE 19. Fill in the measure bars in the following.

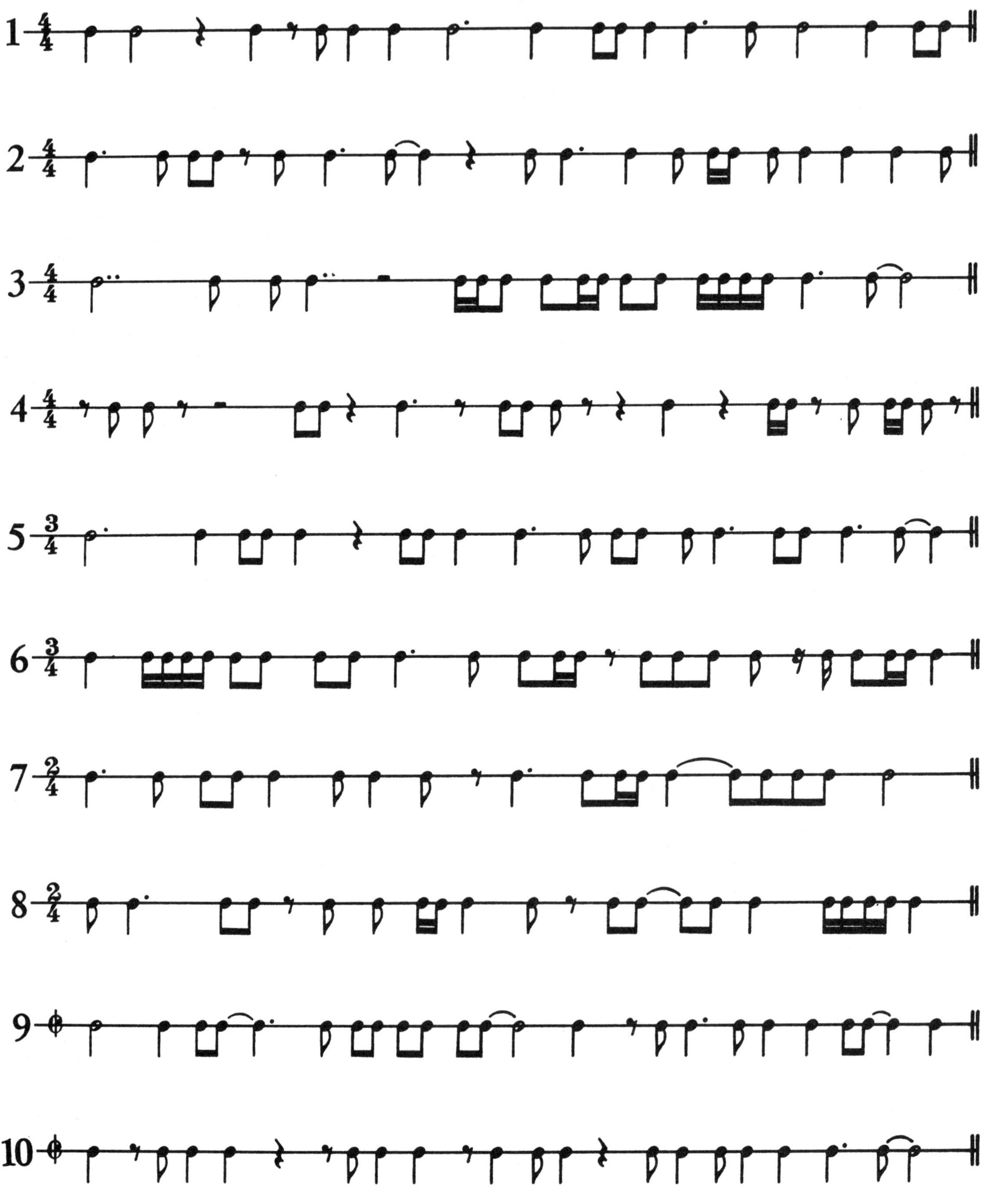

The $\frac{2}{2}$ and ¢ meters correspond relatively to the $\frac{2}{4}$ meter, each having a beat of two in a measure.

$\frac{2}{2}$ or ¢ = $\frac{2}{4}$ = =

Likewise the $\frac{3}{2}$, $\frac{3}{4}$ and $\frac{3}{8}$ are relatively alike, with three beats to a measure.

$\frac{3}{2}$ = $\frac{3}{4}$ = $\frac{3}{8}$ = = = =

However, the beat of any of the preceding meters may be changed according to the speed or feeling of the rhythm. $\frac{3}{4}$ and $\frac{3}{8}$ may have a beat of one in a measure, $\frac{4}{8}$ may have a beat of two, and $\frac{2}{4}$ may have a beat of four, or one, as in a Presto or Galop.

Composers do not always write in the meters best adapted to the speed or tempo of their compositions, but rely on the performer's sense of rhythm and interpretation. (see exercise 22, no. 2)

When a beat of any meter is divided into three parts, it is called a triplet and is written thus:

3 3 3

In each case the triplet consists of three notes of the same denomination that are used when the beat is divided in half.

= = 3

= = 3

= = 3

$\frac{6}{8}$, $\frac{9}{8}$, and $\frac{12}{8}$ meters are usually grouped in triplets.

Some of the subdivisions are:

$\frac{6}{8}$ $\frac{9}{8}$

$\frac{12}{8}$

These three meters may have a beat for each group of triplets, or if taken in a slow tempo, may have a beat for each eighth note. $\frac{6}{4}$ and $\frac{9}{4}$ meters correspond in grouping to the $\frac{6}{8}$ and $\frac{9}{8}$ meters, but usually have a beat for each quarter note.

$\frac{5}{4}$ meter is an odd rhythm and difficult to count. There is a beat for each quarter note, but the stress is sometimes on the first and third quarters and sometimes on the first and fourth. Occasionally we come across a meter with the sixteenth note for the unit. Modern composers are continually inventing new meters. Roy Harris uses a $\frac{7}{8}$ meter in his "Little Suite". Carlos Chavez, in one of his Preludes, uses six different meters (¢ $\frac{5}{4}$ $\frac{1}{2}$ $\frac{3}{4}$ $\frac{3}{2}$ $\frac{6}{4}$) in one movement.

The following terms are used to indicate a fixed tempo, starting with the slowest and finishing with the fastest.

Largo	Moderato
Larghetto	Allegretto
Lento	Allegro
Adagio	Vivace
Andante	Presto
Andantino	Prestissimo

We measure tempo with a metronome, a mechanical or electric clock which may be set at various speeds representing the number of beats to be played at the tempo set by the composer. The approximate metronomic indications for the list above will be found on the face of the metronome. Listen to the metronome at these varying tempos so as to establish a feeling for the time values of each.

EXERCISE 20. Fill in the measure bars in the following.

1 6/8

2 9/8

3 12/8

4 6/4

5 3/2

6 ¢

7 5/4

8 4/8

9 3/8

10 6/8

EXERCISE 21. Complete the time values in each of the following measures, using either notes, rests or dots, according to the space available.

1. 6/8

2. 6/8

3. 9/8

4. 12/8

5. 6/4

6. 3/2

7. 5/4

8. 3/8

9. 3/8

10. 4/8

EXERCISE 22. Study the time values in the following excerpts. Decide how many beats in a measure. Mark where each beat occurs. Sing or play with correct rhythm.

A Phrase is a musical sentence. It is like a line of poetry in a song. Sometimes a Phrase will start on the first beat of a measure and sometimes on an odd beat or fraction of a beat, called a pickup. The Phrase usually finishes on a note of longer duration, or at the end of a rhythmic pattern. A double bar does not necessarily mean the beginning or ending of a Phrase. There are one to four Phrases in each of the preceding excerpts. Determine where each Phrase begins and ends. Place a phrase mark (,) at the end of each phrase. This can be best determined by singing or playing the phrases and feeling where the phrases end. The phrase ends have a feeling of rest or pause.

CHAPTER 4
Intervals

An Interval is the space or relationship between two tones. When applied to a single tone, it refers to the relationship of that tone to a root or fundamental. Intervals are counted upward on the Diatonic Major scale and include both lower and upper notes. That is, if the lower note of any interval is F, the interval is measured by the scale degrees of F Major.

Intervals played or written together are called Harmonic.

Intervals played or written one after another are called Melodic.

INTERVALS IN THE SCALE OF C MAJOR

Sing these intervals by number calling C 1; first as melodic intervals; then divide the class and sing them as harmonic intervals.

In the study of Harmony, we shall find intervals of a Ninth, Tenth, Eleventh and Thirteenth. Intervals of over an octave may have two names. They are sometimes considered as being within the octave. Sing these intervals, then compare them.

Chromatic signs do not affect the number names of intervals. Each of the following is a Third, as three scale degrees are included.

EXERCISE 23. What are the number names of the following intervals? Sing them by number calling the lower tone 1.

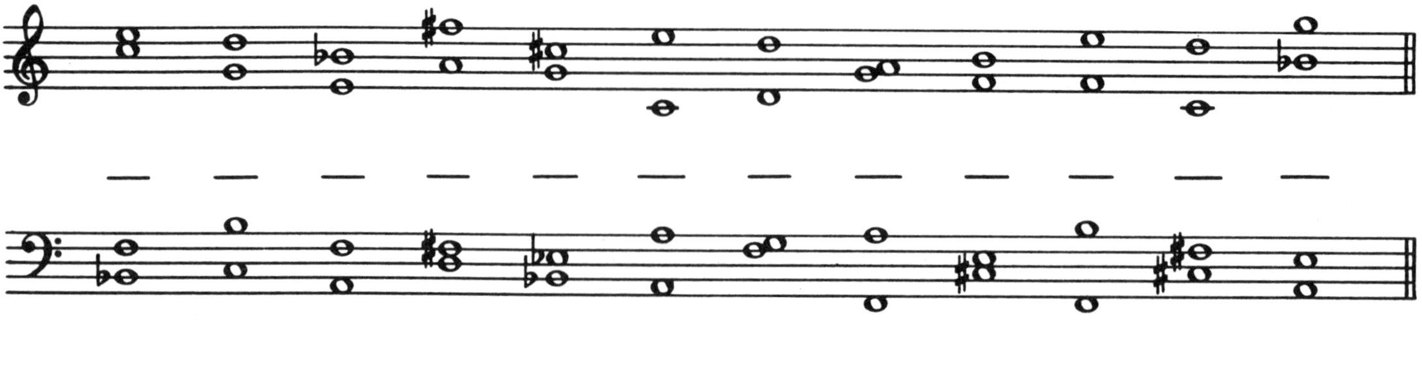

An Interval is Major when the upper note is found in the major scale of the lower note.

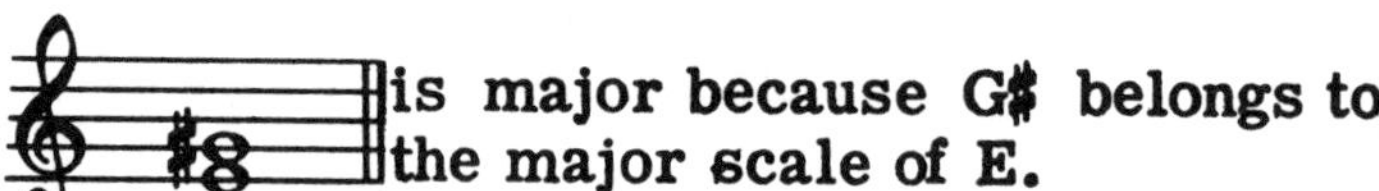

is major because G♯ belongs to the major scale of E.

Sing this interval calling the lower tone 1. Learn to recognize its sound.

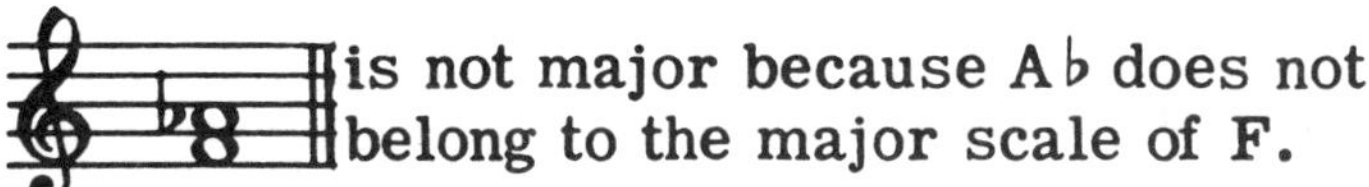
is not major because A♭ does not belong to the major scale of F.

Sing this interval calling the lower tone 1. Notice the difference in quality or tonality.

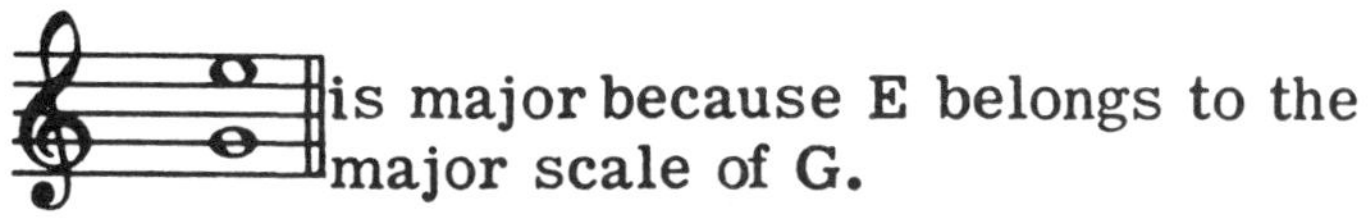
is major because E belongs to the major scale of G.

Sing this interval calling the lower tone 1.

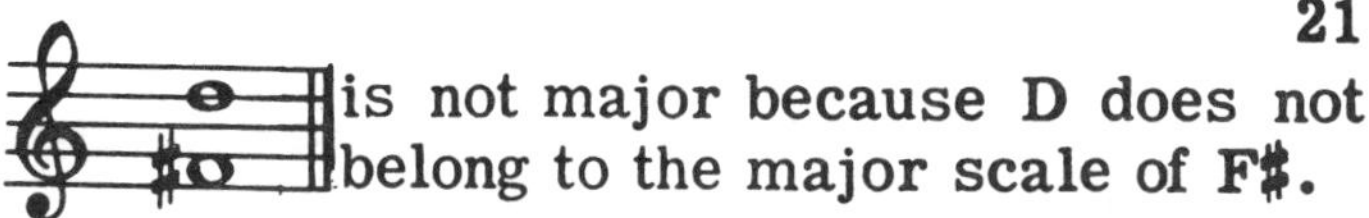
is not major because D does not belong to the major scale of F♯.

Sing this interval calling the lower tone 1. Notice the difference in tonality.

A Minor Interval is a half step smaller than a Major Interval.

Any Major Interval may be made Minor, either by lowering the upper note a half step, or by raising the lower note a half step.

All Seconds, Thirds, Sixths and Sevenths may be either Major or Minor. Primes, Fourths, Fifths and Octaves, which respond to the rule for finding Major intervals, are called Perfect.

EXERCISE 24. Which of the following intervals are perfect?

EXERCISE 25. Which of the following intervals are major and which are minor? Try to identify them also by singing them, calling the lower tone 1.

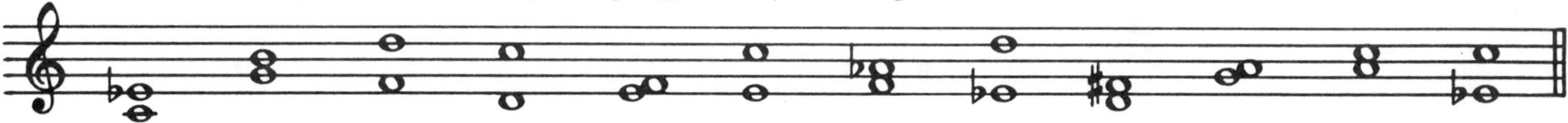

EXERCISE 26. Change the following major intervals to minor.

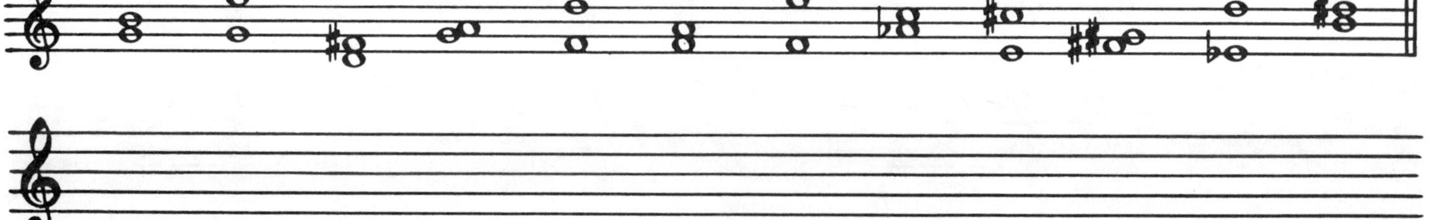

If a Perfect Interval is made a half step larger, it becomes an Augmented Interval. If a Perfect Interval is made a half step smaller, it becomes a Diminished Interval. Sing each of these intervals calling the lower tone 1.

If a Major Interval is made a half step larger it becomes Augmented. Sing them.

If a Minor Interval is made a half step smaller, it becomes Diminished.

All augmented and diminished intervals are enharmonic with the next larger or smaller intervals. Sing these intervals.

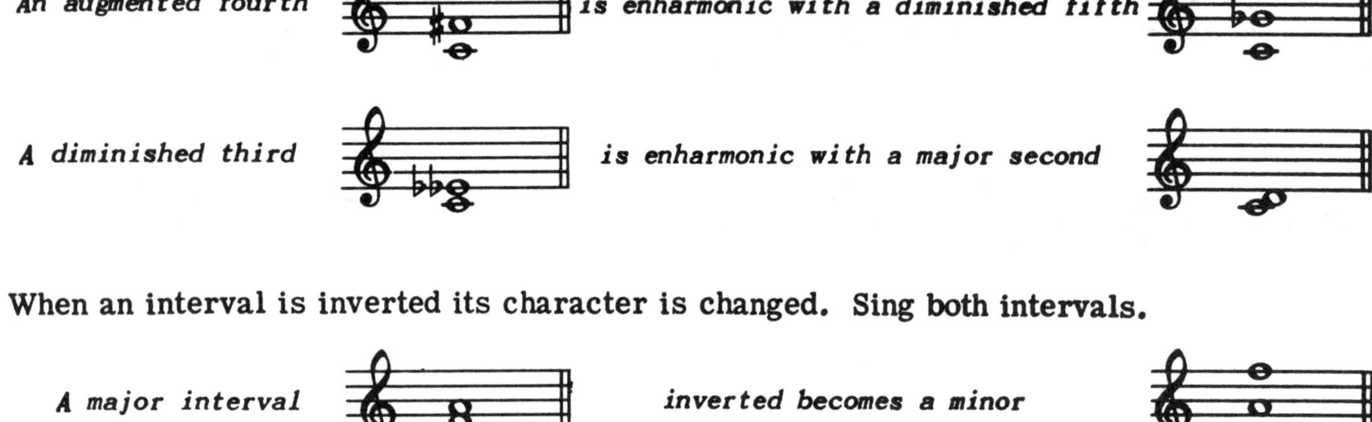

When an interval is inverted its character is changed. Sing both intervals.

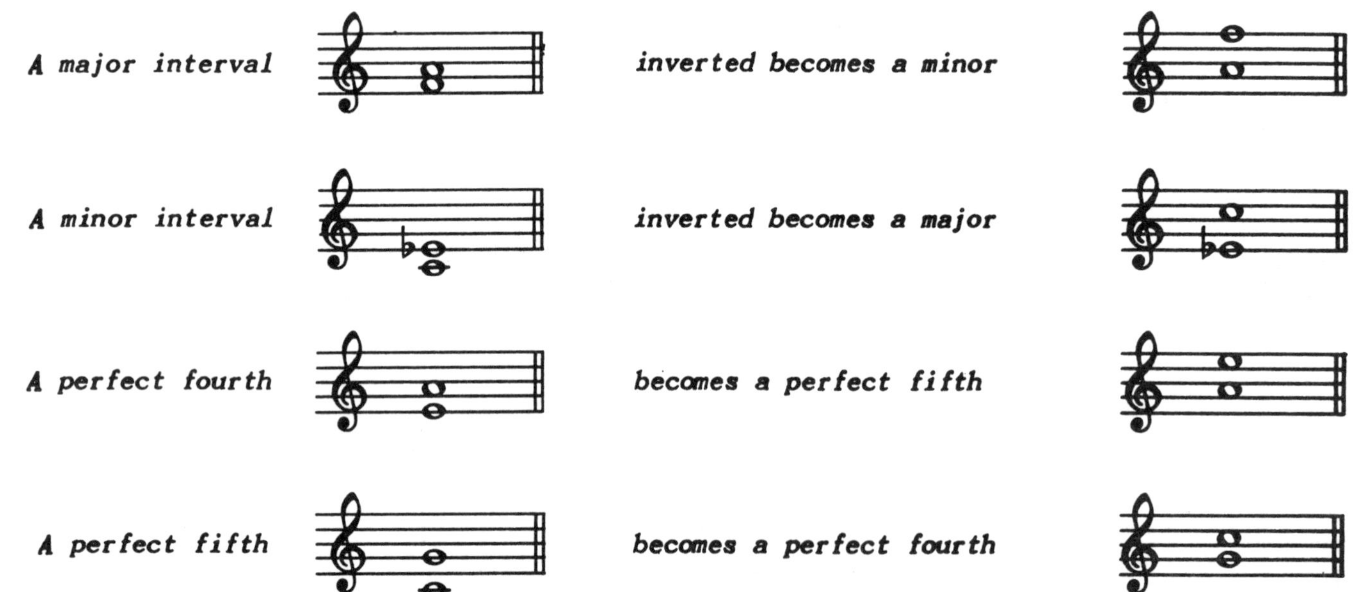

EXERCISE 27. Write five examples of each of the following intervals. MINOR THIRD: MAJOR SECOND: MINOR SIXTH: MAJOR SEVENTH.

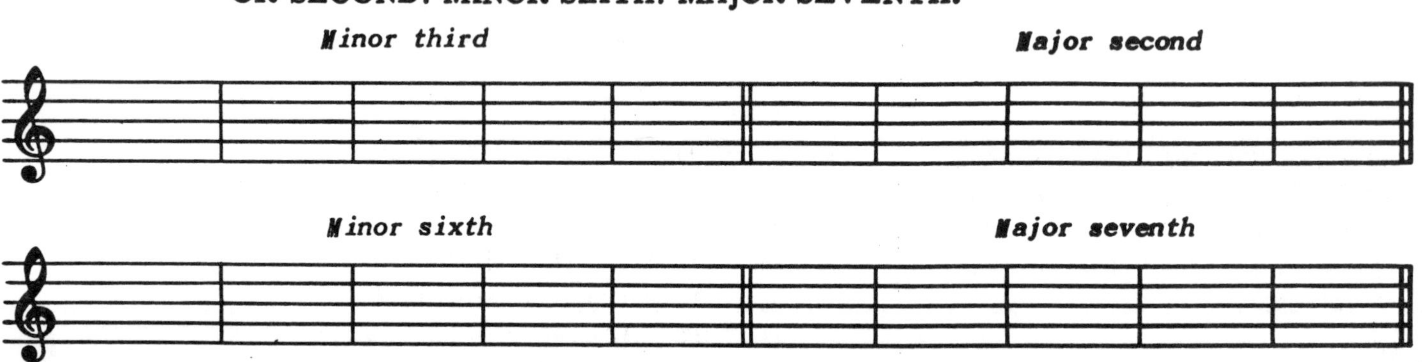

EXERCISE 28. Change each perfect fourth or fifth to an augmented fourth or fifth. Sing all these intervals as written and as augmented.

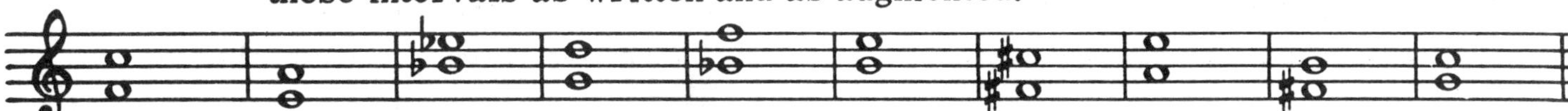

EXERCISE 29. Change each perfect fourth or fifth to a diminished fourth or fifth. Sing all these intervals as written and as diminished.

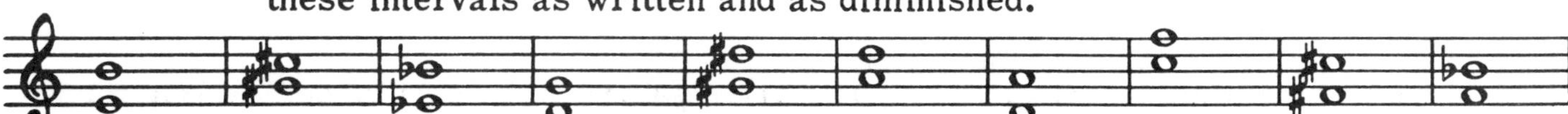

EXERCISE 30. Name each of the following intervals.

EXERCISE 31. Write the inversion of each of the following intervals and name it.

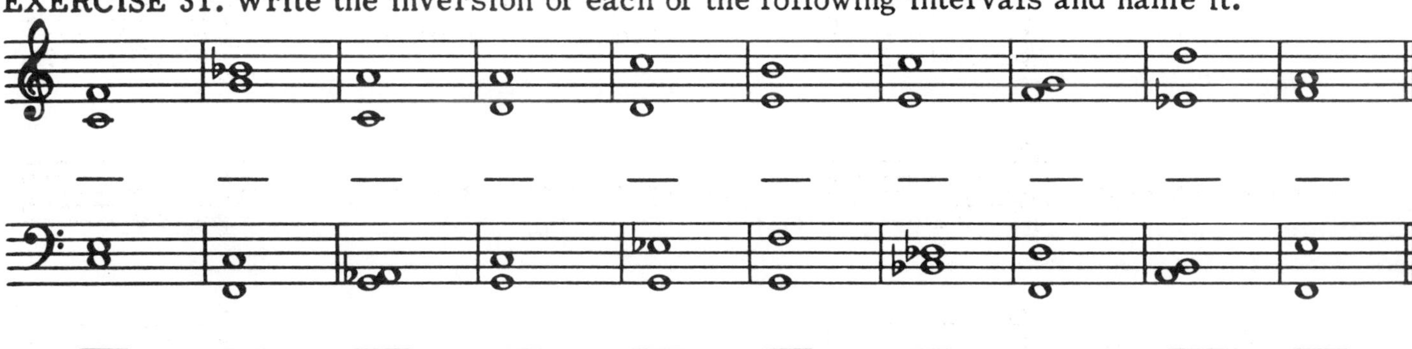

EXERCISE 32. Name the following intervals which have the upper note in the treble and the lower note in the bass.

The augmented fourth and the diminished fifth have a strong tendency to move to the nearest tones of the tonic chord. The movement of a tone towards a point of rest is called resolution.

An augmented interval usually resolves to an interval larger than itself.

A diminished interval usually resolves to an interval smaller than itself.

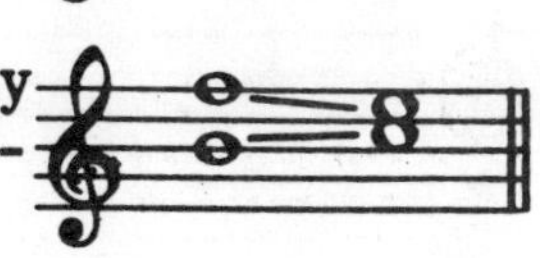

CHAPTER 5
Tonic and Dominant Triads

Each scale degree has a name as well as a number.

The first degree, which gives the tone of the key, is called the Tonic. Nearly every composition ends with some arrangement of the 1-3-5 chord, with the Tonic in the bass. This expresses the feeling of finality or ending. The fifth degree is the dominating note of the scale, and is called the Dominant. Its chord in some form usually precedes the final Tonic chord. The fourth degree is called the Subdominant. These three degrees are usually referred to by name.

The names of all the scale degrees are as follows:

First Degree - Tonic
Second Degree - Supertonic
Third Degree - Mediant
Fourth Degree - Subdominant
Fifth Degree - Dominant
Sixth Degree - Submediant
Seventh Degree - Leading Tone
Eighth Degree - Octave

EXERCISE 33. Write the Tonic and Dominant Triads in the major scales of: G, F, D, B♭, A. Do not use signatures, but set a sharp or flat before each note which requires one.

A Triad is a chord composed of three notes: a root, its third, and its fifth. Triads can be built on any scale degree. A Roman numeral indicates the chord whose root is that degree-

Here are the Triads in the major scale of C.

In this chapter we will consider only Tonic and Dominant Triads. The triad on the first degree, I, is composed of a root, a major third and perfect fifth, and is called the Tonic Triad. The triad on the fifth degree, V, is composed of a root, a major third and a perfect fifth, and is called the Dominant Triad. Triads are Major when they contain a major third and a perfect fifth. They are Minor when they contain a minor third and a perfect fifth. In the major scale, Major Triads occur on the first, fourth and fifth degrees. Minor Triads occur on the second, third and sixth degrees. A diminished Triad occurs on the seventh degree. (See chapter 16)

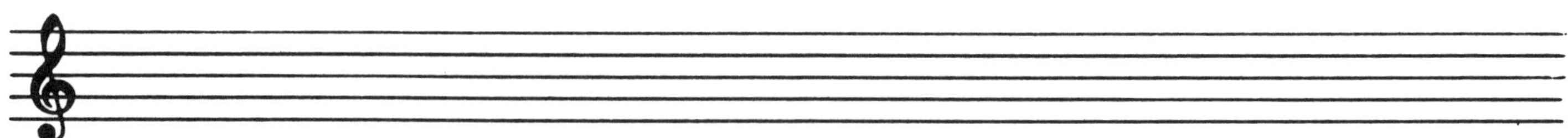

Chords may be written in different positions. The original position always has the root at the bottom. Other positions are called Inversions.

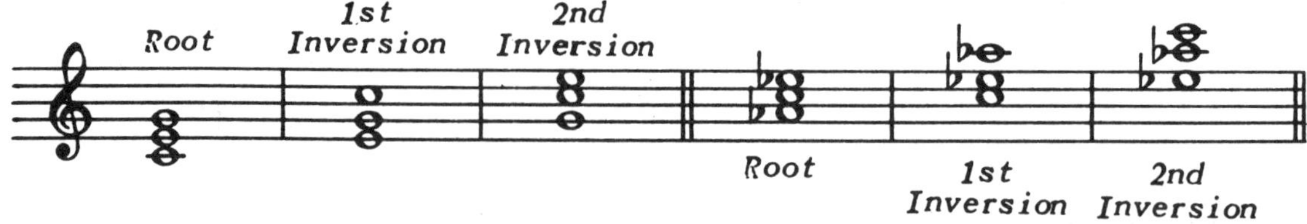

EXERCISE 34. Write the three positions of the Tonic Triads in the keys of G, F, D, B♭, A, E♭, E. Do not use signatures.

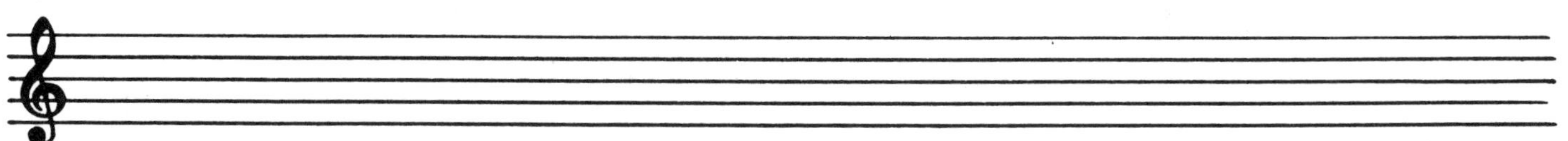

Harmony in a simple form is usually represented by four voices or parts. The root of each chord may be written in the bass, with the three upper voices in the treble. As there are only three tones in the Tonic and Dominant chords, one of these tones must be doubled. The root is the tone most often doubled. The movement of one chord to another is called Progression.

Divide the class and sing these progressions as a chorus. Try to recognize them by ear.

In many progressions there is a common tone. It is usually better to keep the common tone in the same voice.

EXERCISE 35. Complete the following progressions, using the nearest positions of the upper voices.

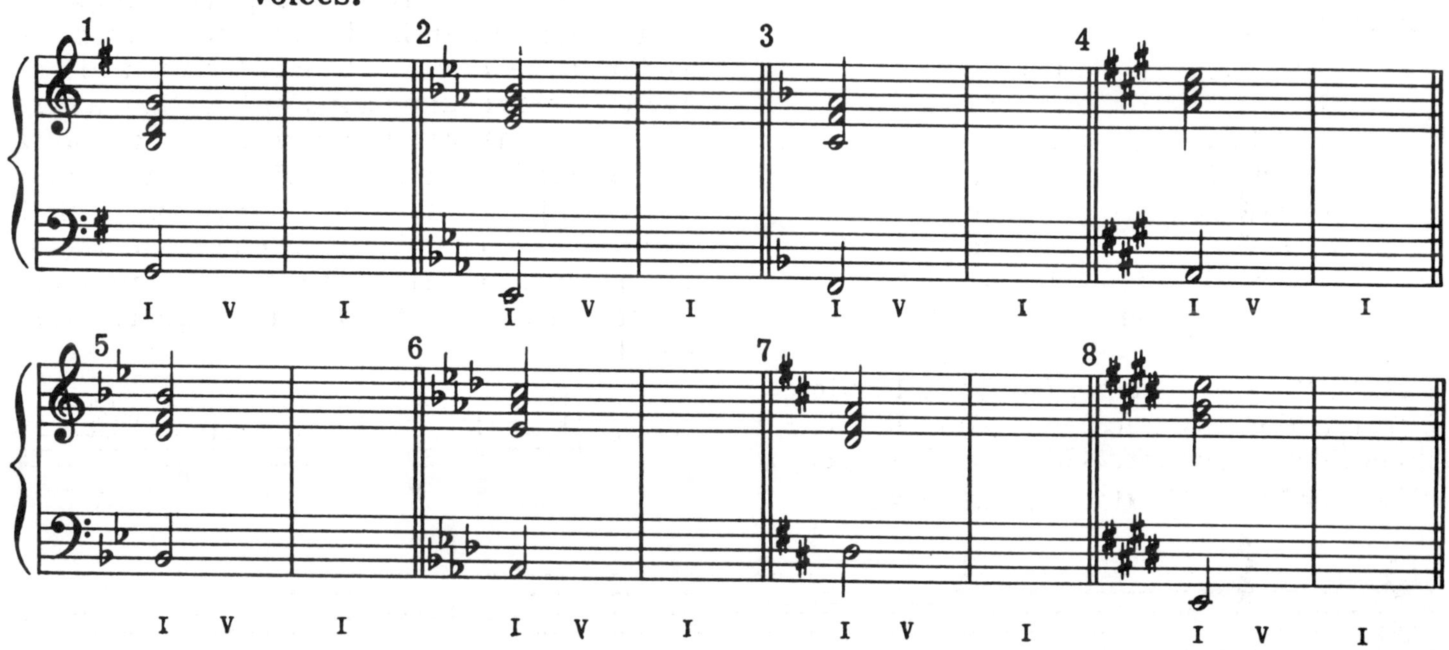

A cadence is the close or end of a phrase. The chord ending V to I, is called Authentic. When the root of the Tonic chord is in the top voice, it is called Perfect. If the third or fifth of the Tonic chord is in the top voice, it is called Imperfect. Sing these cadence chords. Try to recognize them by ear.

EXERCISE 36. State which of the cadences you have written in Exercise 35 are perfect and which are imperfect.

Almost every melody implies harmony, Take the melody:

There are a number of ways in which this melody can be harmonized. But if we use only the two chords we have been studying, it would look like this:

Sing this phrase as a chorus. Try to recognize the chords by ear.

EXERCISE 37. Harmonize the following melodies.

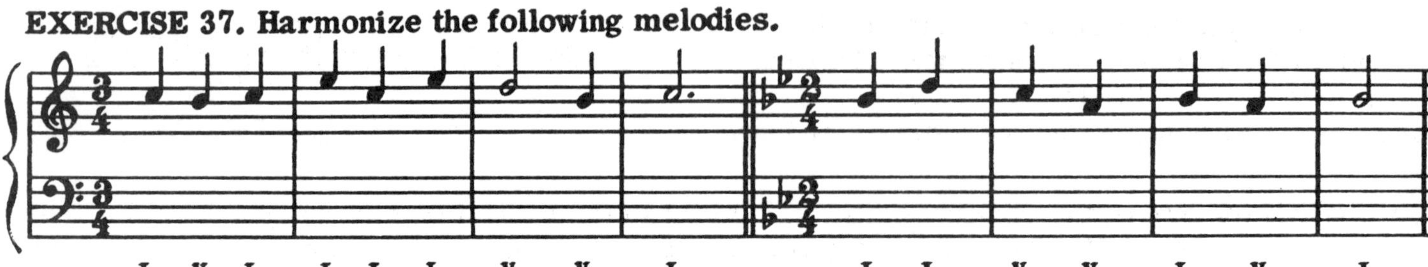

When a melody note repeats, it is usually better to change the chord. Sing this progression. Try to recognize the chords by ear.

EXERCISE 38. Harmonize the following melodies.

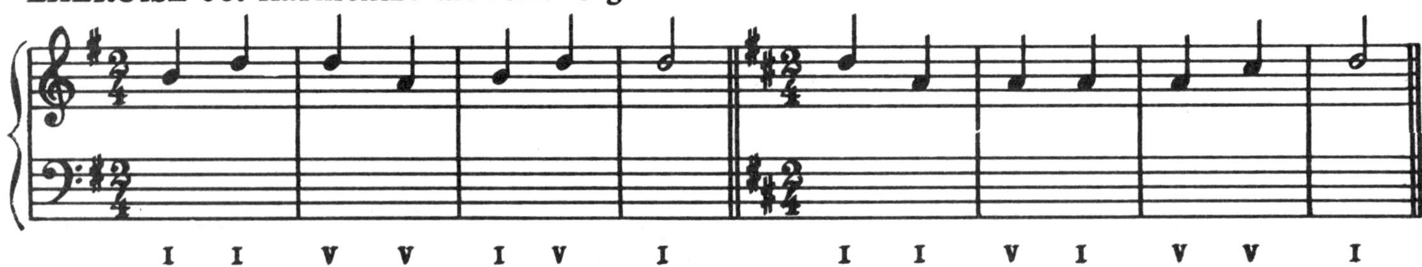

A chord that is introduced on the last beat of a measure is usually not repeated on the first beat of the next measure.

EXERCISE 39. Harmonize the following melodies.

I I V I I I V I V I I I I V I V V V I

CHAPTER 6
The Dominant Seventh Chord

The Dominant Seventh chord is formed by adding the minor seventh interval to the Dominant Triad.

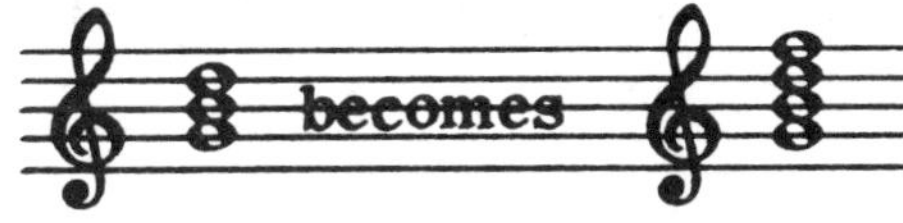

Therefore, it contains a root, a major third, a perfect fifth and a minor seventh. The Dominant Seventh chord belongs to the key of which it is the Dominant, and gets its name not because it contains the seventh degree of the scale, but because it contains the seventh interval above its root, the Dominant. This chord is indicated by the Roman numeral V for Dominant and the Arabic 7 at the right to express the seventh interval.

EXERCISE 40. Write the dominant seventh chords in the following major keys. F, G, B♭, E♭, A, E, D♭. Do not use signatures, but put the name of the key at the left, as in the above example.

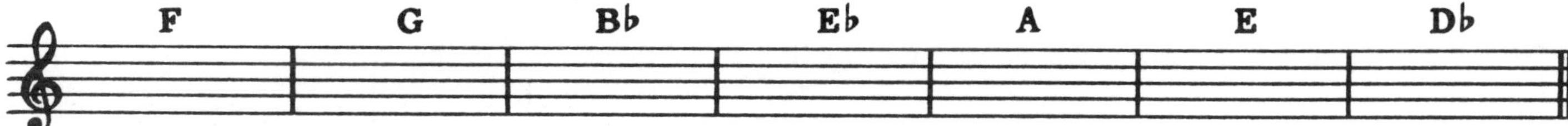

Dominant Seventh chords may be written in different positions. Here are various positions of the Dominant Seventh of G. Name the inversions.

EXERCISE 41. Write four positions of the dominant seventh in the following keys. Do not use signatures.

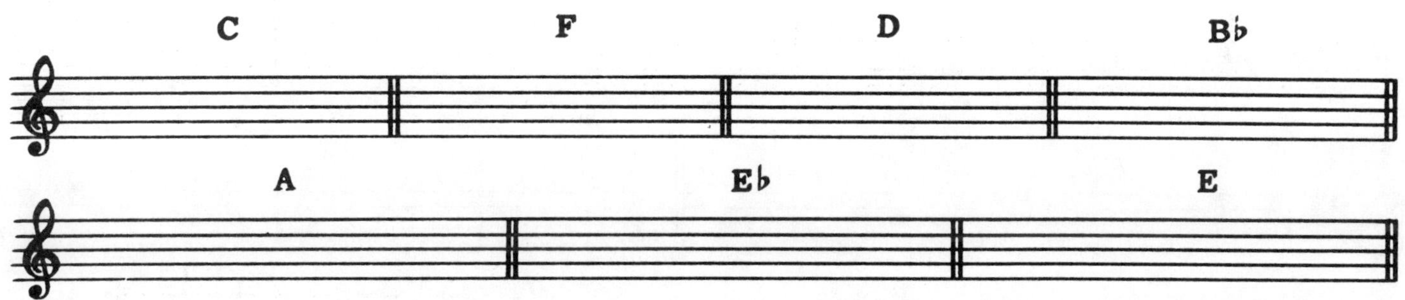

In three part harmony, the fifth of the chord is omitted. In four part harmony, the fifth is sometimes omitted, making the chord easier to resolve. Thinking in the degrees of the Tonic key, in resolving the Dominant Seventh chord, seven moves to one, four moves to three, and five remains stationary. (Sing these resolutions. Try to recognize the chords by ear.

When all the tones of a chord are as close as possible, (usually within the octave) it is called Close Harmony. When the tones are spread, it is called Open Harmony. The resolution of the Dominant Seventh chord is the same in either case.

EXERCISE 42. Resolve the following Dominant Seventh chords. Name the key and figure both chords as in the example.

The root of the Dominant Seventh chord may be written in the bass, and is usually doubled in the upper voices. Sing these progressions. Name them by ear after hearing them on the piano.

The Dominant Triad sometimes precedes the Dominant Seventh. The Dominant Seventh may be repeated in a different position before resolving. Sing these resolutions. Name these chords by ear after hearing them on the piano.

EXERCISE 43. Complete the following progressions. Use the nearest position of each chord and keep the common tone in the same voice.

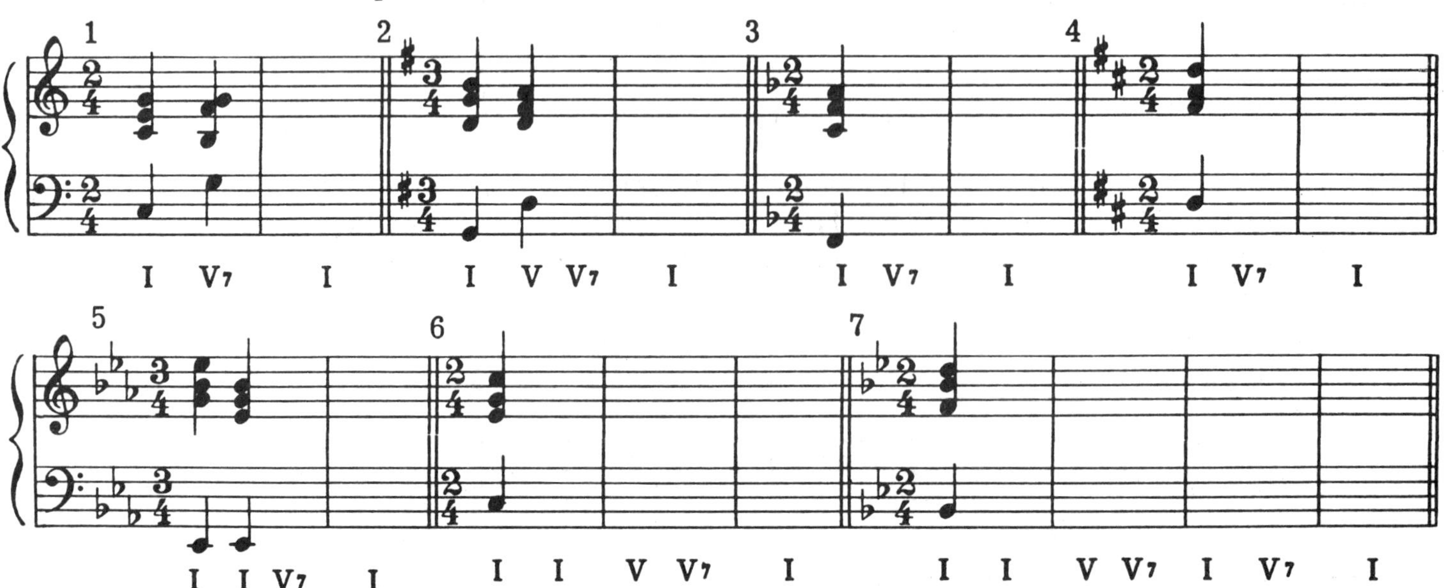

On account of the minor seventh interval, the Dominant Seventh chord is more strongly attracted than the Dominant Triad, towards the Tonic. It is therefor used more often to precede the Tonic at the end of a phrase. A phrase will seldom end with the Dominant Seventh chord, but will often end with the Dominant Triad, if another phrase follows.

EXERCISE 44. Harmonize the following melodies. State the reason for your choice between Dominant Triads and Dominant Seventh chords.

1

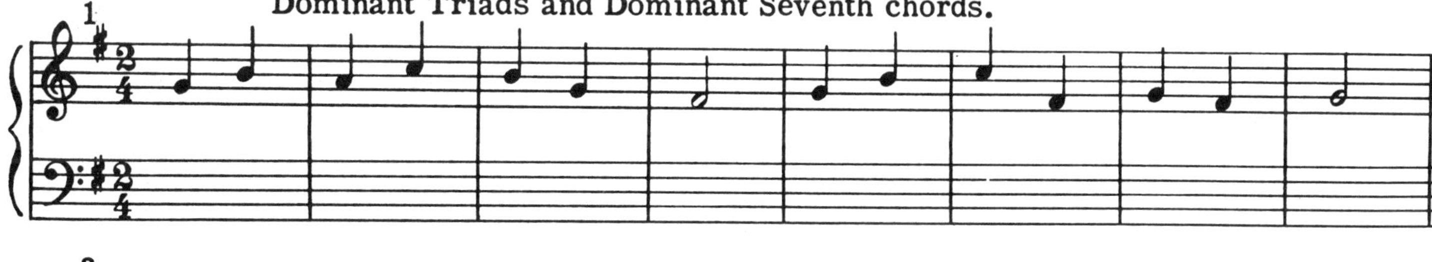

2

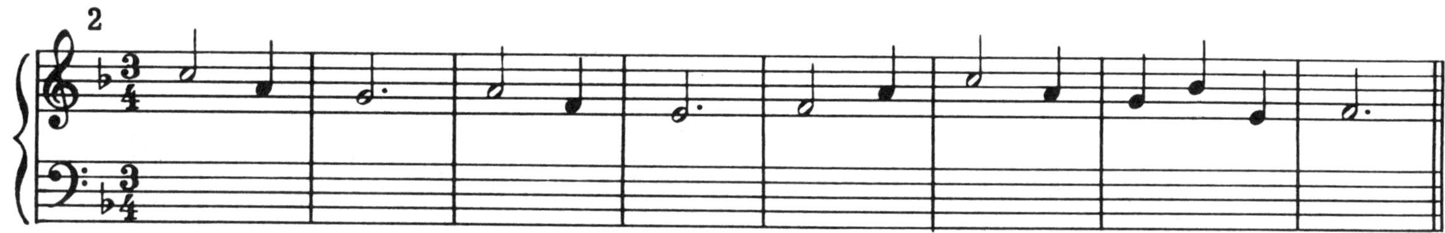

In modern composition and arranging, there is a tendency to use full harmony and to disregard the resolution of each separate voice. In the following examples, the first conforms to the rule for perfect resolution, but the others do not. Can you tell why? Sing these resolutions to find out.

EXERCISE 45. Harmonize the following melodies.

1

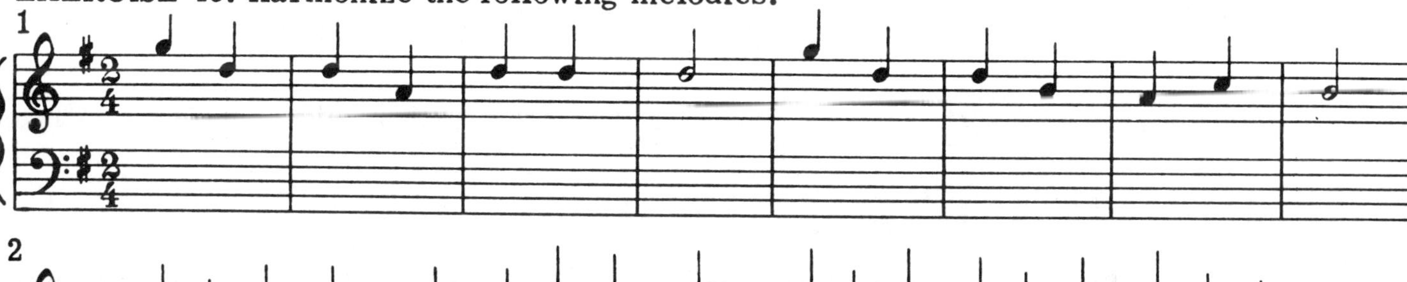

2

In harmonizing the melody on the second scale degree, the Dominant Seventh chord appears complete with all four notes. The bass may be held over for the repetition of a chord, or lowered an octave. Sing these progressions and name the chords by ear after hearing them played on the piano.

EXERCISE 46. Harmonize the following melody.

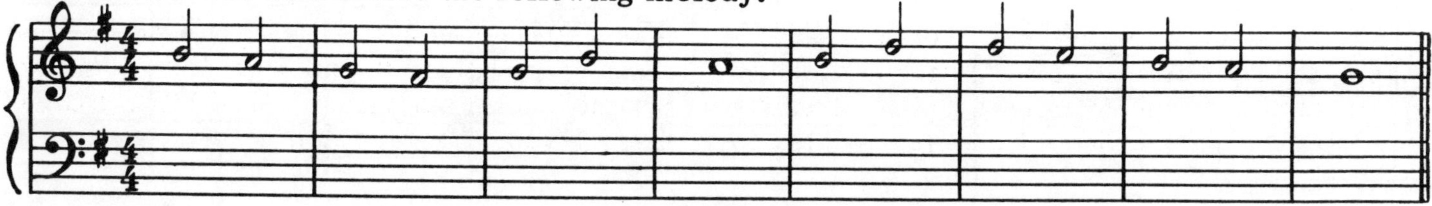

CHAPTER 7
The Subdominant Triad

The Subdominant Triad is built on the fourth degree, IV, of the scale. It contains a root, major third and perfect fifth. The chord ending IV to I is called the Plagal Cadence. When the root of the Tonic chord is in the top voice, it is called Perfect. If the third or fifth of the Tonic chord is in the top voice, it is called Imperfect. Sing these progressions and name the chords. You will find this cadence in hymns.

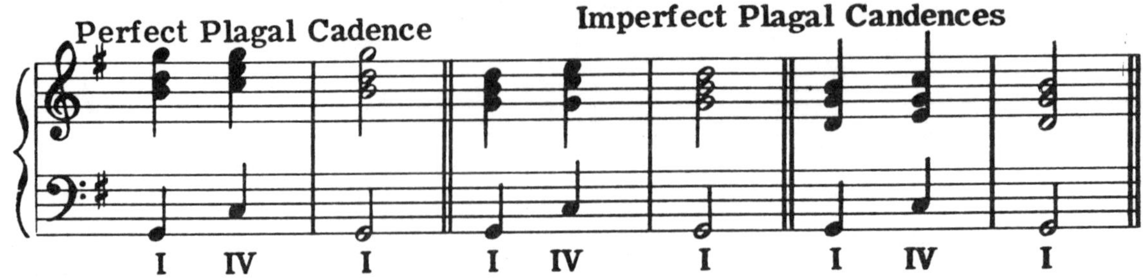

EXERCISE 47. Complete the following Plagal Cadences and state which are Perfect and which are Imperfect.

EXERCISE 48. Complete the following Cadences and state whether Authentic or Plagal, Perfect or Imperfect.

The Subdominant Triad may progress to the Dominant or Dominant Seventh. Sing these progressions and name the chords by ear after hearing them played at the piano.

EXERCISE 49. Harmonize the following melodies.

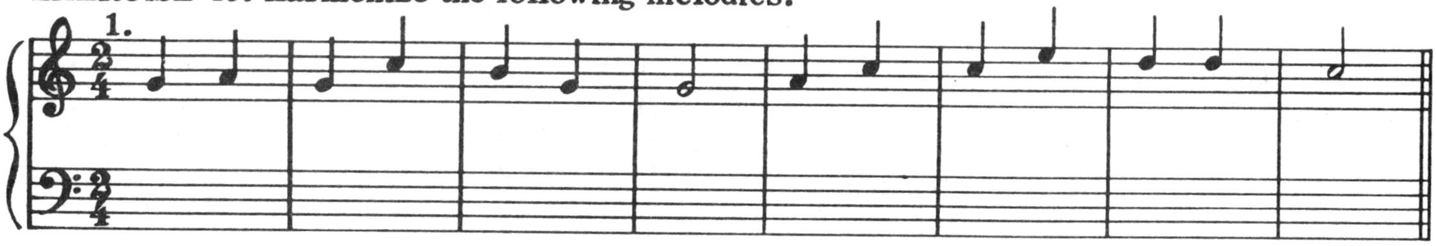

1.

2.

3.

In the above melodies you have a choice of chords in several places. Remember, when a melody note repeats, it is usually better to change the chord.

A chord is Inverted when any note other than the root is in the bass. When the fifth of any triad is in the bass, it is called a Six-Four chord. It takes its name from the intervals of which it is composed. In the following example, the intervals are, a sixth from the bass note G to the note E, and a fourth from the bass note G to the note C. All intervals are considered as being within the octave. The fifth is doubled in the upper voices.

SECOND INVERSION

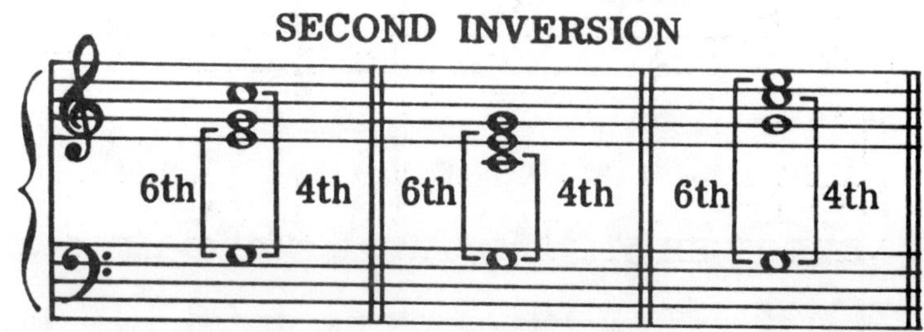

Arabic numerals are placed at the right of the Roman numeral, or over the bass note, to indicate this chord inversion. This chord is used most frequently to precede either the Dominant Triad or Dominant Seventh. It is sometimes written as the I_2 chord. The Arabic number represents the second inversion. Sing this progression. Name the chords after hearing them played on the piano.

EXERCISE 50. Harmonize the following melodies.

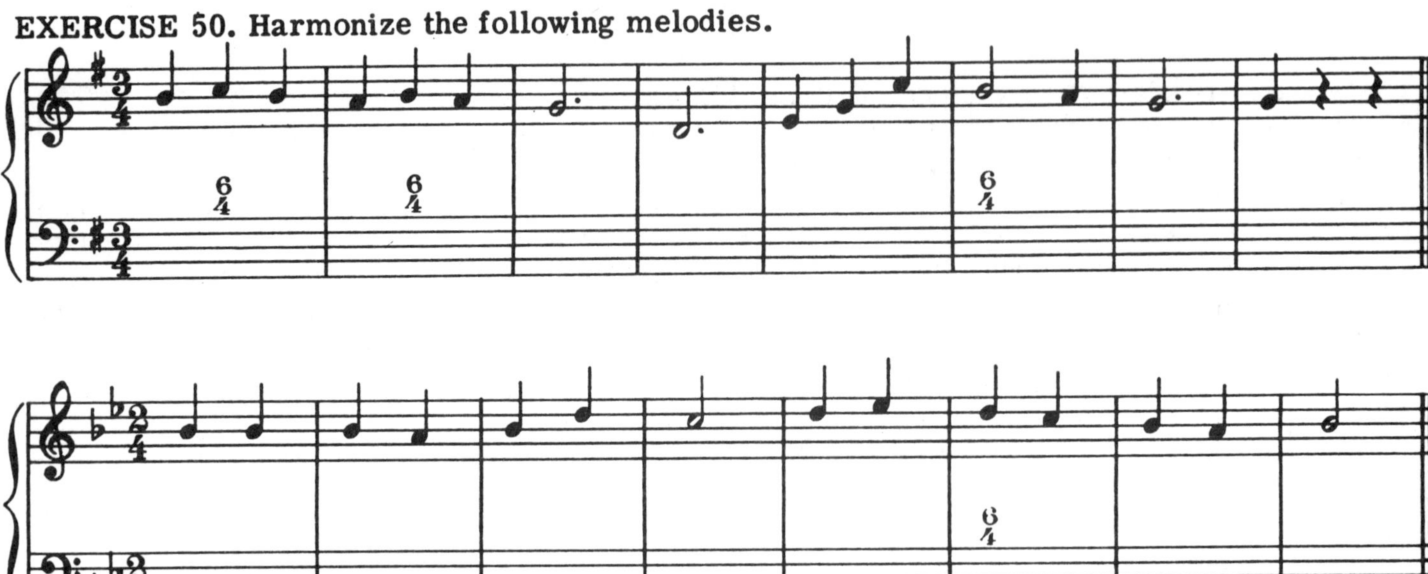

When the third of any triad is in the bass, it is called a Chord of the Sixth or a Six-Three chord, because of the intervals it contains.

FIRST INVERSION

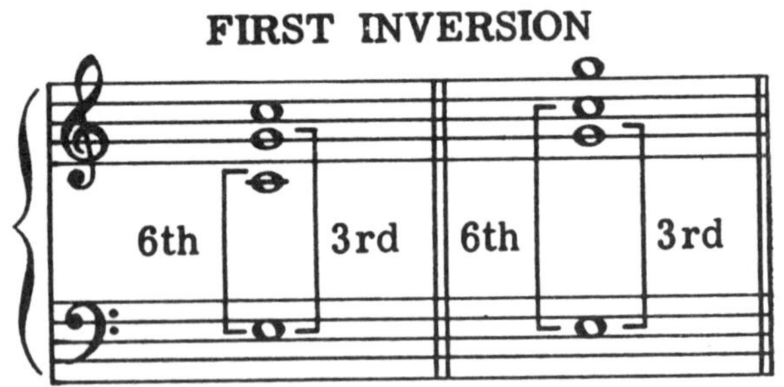

In this inversion the third is seldom doubled. Either the root or fifth is doubled in the upper voices. This chord is sometimes figured with one Arabic numeral I_6 and sometimes with both I^6_3. Sing this progression. Name the chords.

It may also be written as I_1 chord, the Arabic number representing the first inversion.

EXERCISE 51. Harmonize the following melodies.

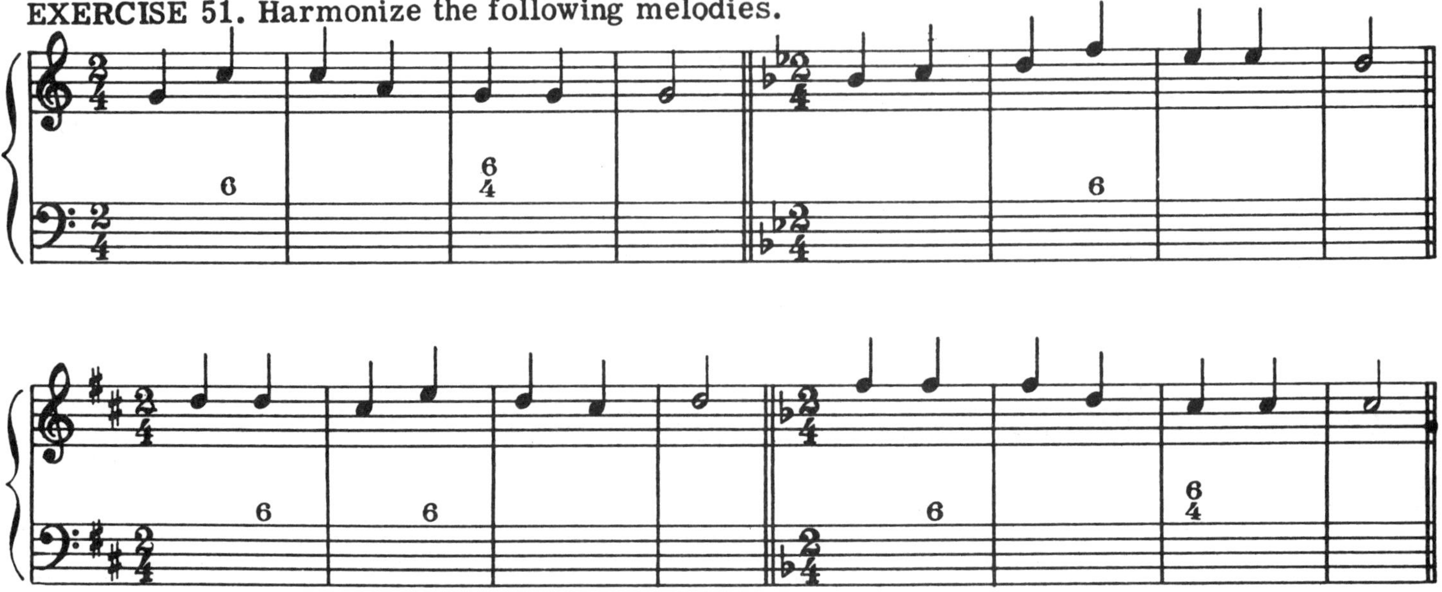

CHAPTER 8
Ear Training

Intervals are classified by their sound. All Perfect Intervals are called Perfect Consonances. Major and minor thirds and sixths are called Imperfect Consonances. All other Intervals are called Dissonances. It is important that these intervals be recognized by their sound. Perfect Consonances are the easiest to recognize. They have a smooth hollow sound. Listen to the following Fourths, Fifths and Octaves. Observe each interval as it is played. Compare the distance between the tones. Sing these intervals. Name them by ear after hearing them played on the piano. Call the lower tone 1, and measure the interval distance when singing.

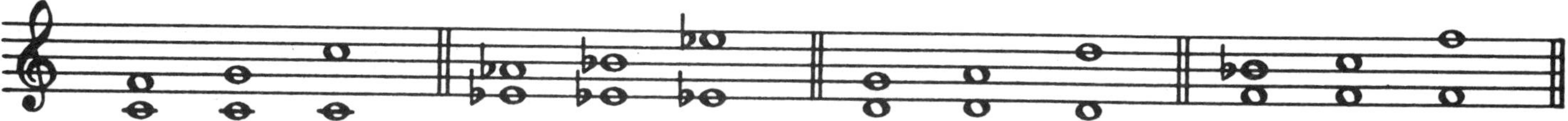

Imperfect Consonances are not quite as easy to recognize. Observe them closely while being played and fix the distance between the tones firmly in your mind. Their sound is not as smooth as Perfect Intervals, but is still not dissonant. Sing them first, then name them.

EXERCISE 52. Close your book while the following Intervals are played and try to name them by ear. First decide if they are Perfect or Imperfect Consonances. If Perfect, are they Fourths, Fifths or Octaves? If Imperfect, are they Thirds or Sixths, and finally are they Major or Minor? Sing them first, then name them.

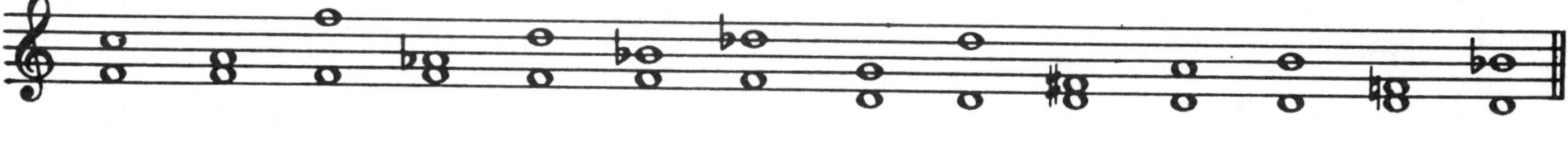

EXERCISE 53. Now try to name by ear Intervals in the pitch of the bass instruments. The lower you go the harder it is to distinguish them. Sing these first before trying to name them.

The Dissonances include Major and Minor Seconds and Sevenths, and all the Augmented and Diminished Intervals. In this chapter we will only consider Seconds and Sevenths.

EXERCISE 54. Name by ear the following Intervals, when played. Sing the intervals also.

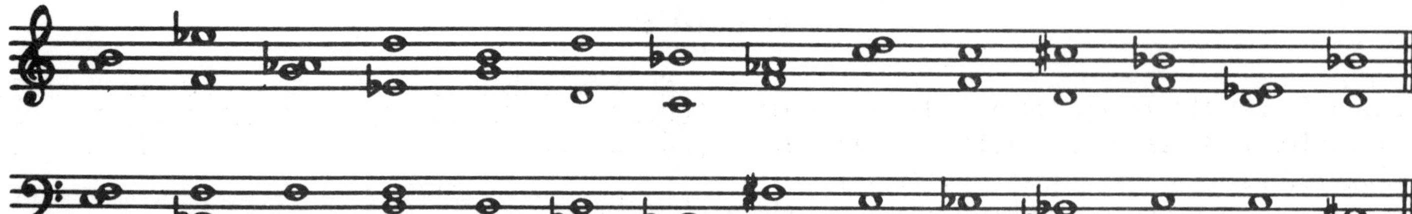

Now we come to chords. All Major and Minor Triads are Consonant because they contain Consonant Intervals. Dominant Sevenths are Dissonant because they contain a Minor Seventh Interval. The difference in sound between Major and Minor Triads should be easily distinguished. Observe the distance between each tone as the following Triads are played. In the Minor Triads the Third is a half step lower. Sing these chords and listen to the moving voice that changes the chord from major to minor.

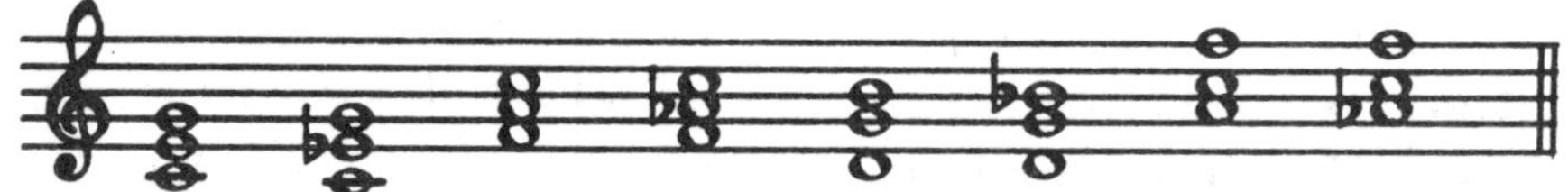

EXERCISE 55. Close your book and state, by ear when played, whether the following Triads are Major or Minor.

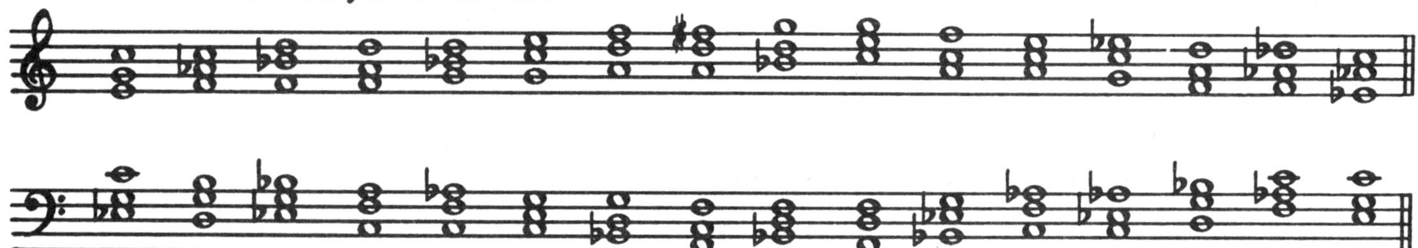

Observe the following Dominant Seventh chords as they are played. Notice the various positions of each chord.

You have learned that the Fifth is often omitted in resolving the Dominant Seventh chord. Now observe the same chords as they are played with the Fifth omitted.

EXERCISE 56. Close your book and state, by ear when played, whether the following chords are Major or Minor Triads, or Dominant Sevenths complete or with the Fifth omitted.

CHAPTER 9
Overtones

Sound is caused by air waves set in motion by vibration. In the human voice, the vibrating bodies are the vocal chords. In wind instruments, the vibrating bodies are the reeds or the lips of the performer. In string instruments, the vibrating bodies are the strings.

The shorter the string or other medium of sound, the more rapid are the vibrations, and the higher is the pitch. The shortest string on a piano vibrates 4186 times a second. The longest string vibrates 27.5 times a second.

Every musical tone is a mixture of sounds made up of a fundamental tone and its Harmonics or Overtones, all sounding together.

If this C is played, it produces the following overtones as well as its own tone.

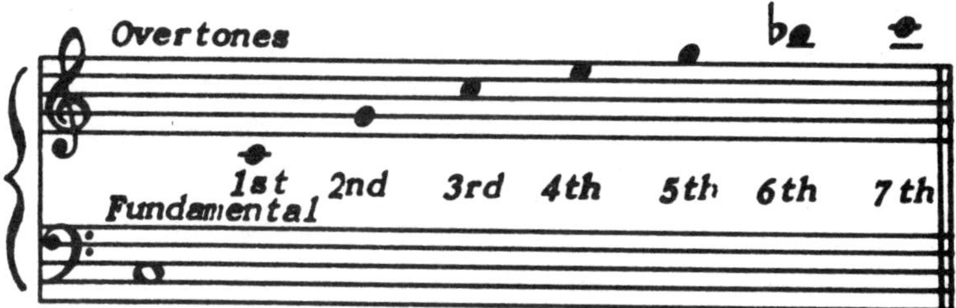

The reason for this is, that a string vibrating as a whole divides itself into halves, thirds, quarters, fifths, etc. indefintely, with each part vibrating proportionately faster and producing its own tone.

Harmonics or Overtones can be sounded separately on certain wind instruments by regulating the lip pressure. These are the so called Open Tones of the brass instruments. On the saxophone, the first overtone is produced with the aid of an octave key. On the clarinet, the second overtone is produced, raising the register an octave and a fifth.

Any tone can be taken as a fundamental, and the overtones will be produced in the same relationship.

There are higher overtones produced by still smaller subdivisions of the string, with the interval between each two tones becoming smaller and smaller, But these higher overtones are too faint to be easily heard.

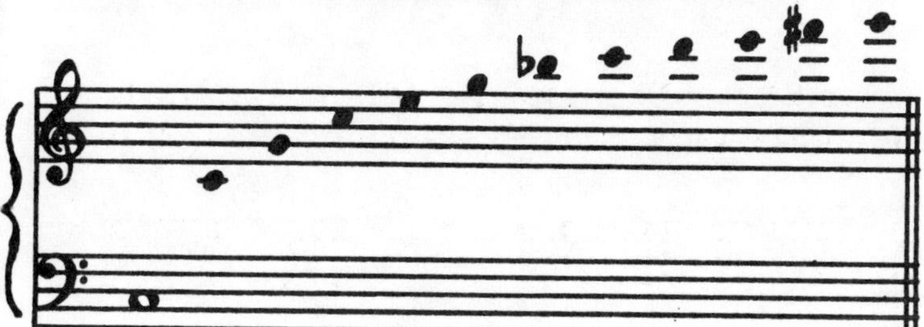

These overtones constitute the Scale of Nature and True Intonation. They are not accurately represented by our present system of equal temperament. The scale of True Intonation could only be employed when modulation was absent. It allowed only the simplest chord changes. Sharps and flats which are now enharmonic, were entirely different tones. True Intonation with its varying intervals, while fitted for the human voice or the violin, could not be employed on a keyed instrument. Hence the Tempered Scale. The octave is the only true interval now employed.

This was divided into twelve equal semitones, allowing modulation into all keys. The Tempered Scale is close enough to true intonation not to shock the ear. However the interval of the major third is an exception, and causes the major triad to sound harsh. Hence the reason for not doubling the third in the first inversion.

A vibrating body has the power to set in motion any other body which vibrates at exactly the same rate of speed. This is called Sympathetic Vibration.

Pitch is the rate of vibration, the acuteness or gravity of sound. Standard Pitch is the rate of vibration of the note A  established for common use. Since the days of Handel. Standard Pitch has varied from 416 vibrations per second to 440. In this country a standard of 435 was established in 1891. It was called International Pitch, as it coincided with the French standard. Today the standard pitch is 440.

CHAPTER 10

Inversions of the Dominant Seventh

The first inversion of the Dominant Seventh has the third in the bass. The Second inversion has the fifth in the bass, and the third inversion has the seventh in the bass. Arabic numerals are placed over the bass note to indicate each inversion. As with inverted triads, all intervals are considered as being within the octave. The third inversion is sometimes figured $^4_2$ and sometimes $_2$. It is also written as the V_3 indicating the third inversion.

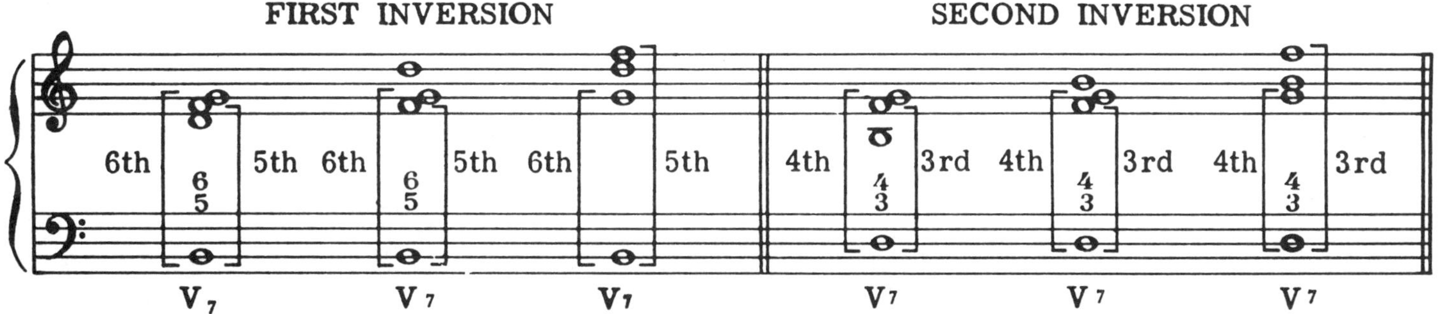

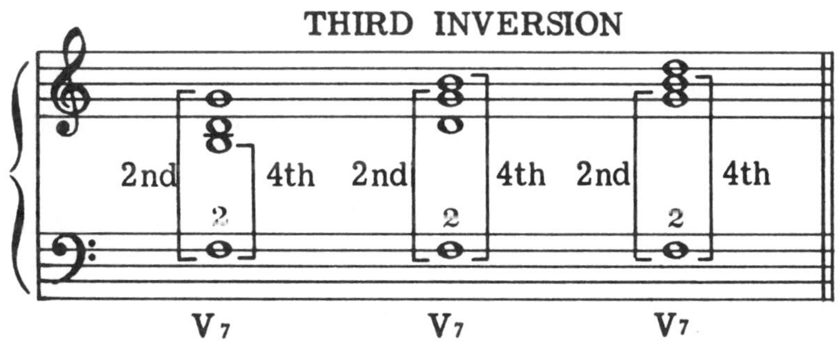

Inversions of the Dominant Seventh afford an excellent opportunity for the use of contrary or oblique motion. Sing the progressions. Name the chords as they are played indicating the inversions.

EXERCISE 57. Fill in the two lower treble parts.

EXERCISE 58. Fill in the two lower treble parts.

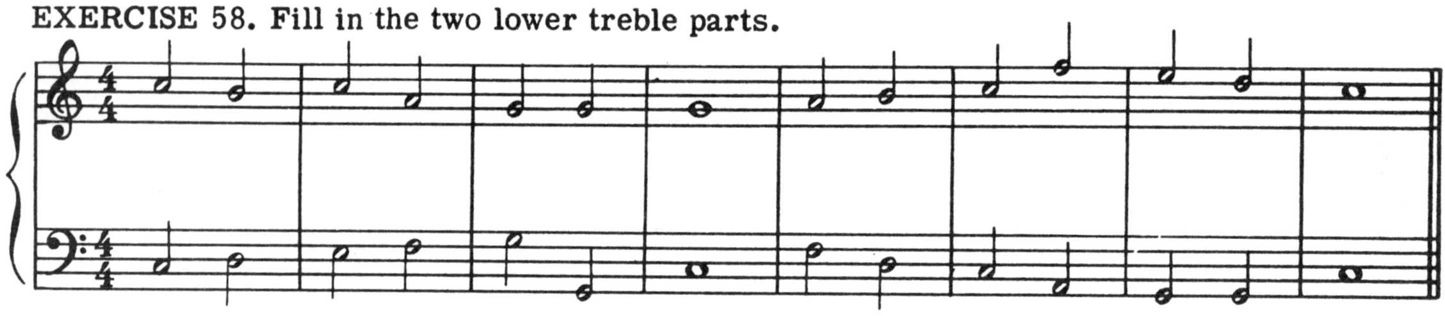

EXERCISE 59. Fill in the two lower treble parts.

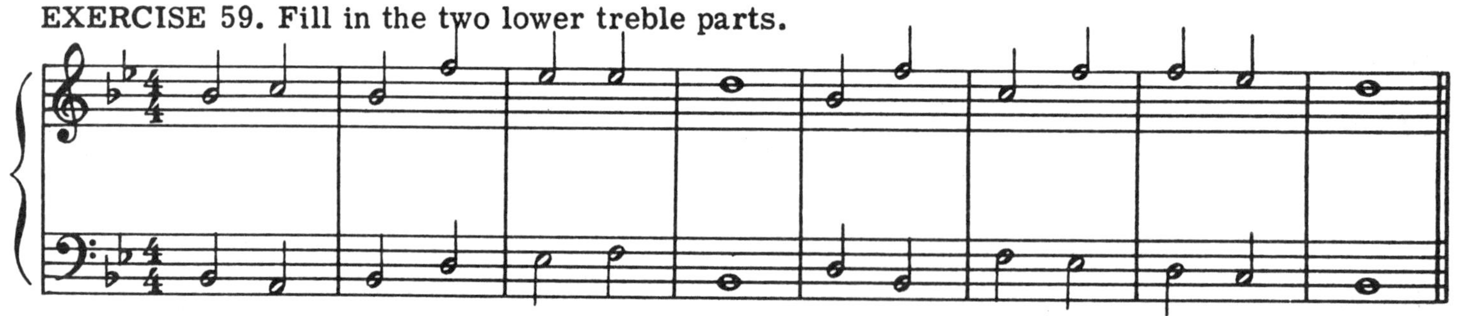

EXERCISE 60. Harmonize the following melody.

Parallel motion is sometimes effective, but parallel octaves are usually avoided, particularly between the bass and melody notes. Sing these progressions. Then name the chords as they are played, indicating the inversions.

EXERCISE 61. Harmonize the following bass passages.

EXERCISE 62. Harmonize the following melody.

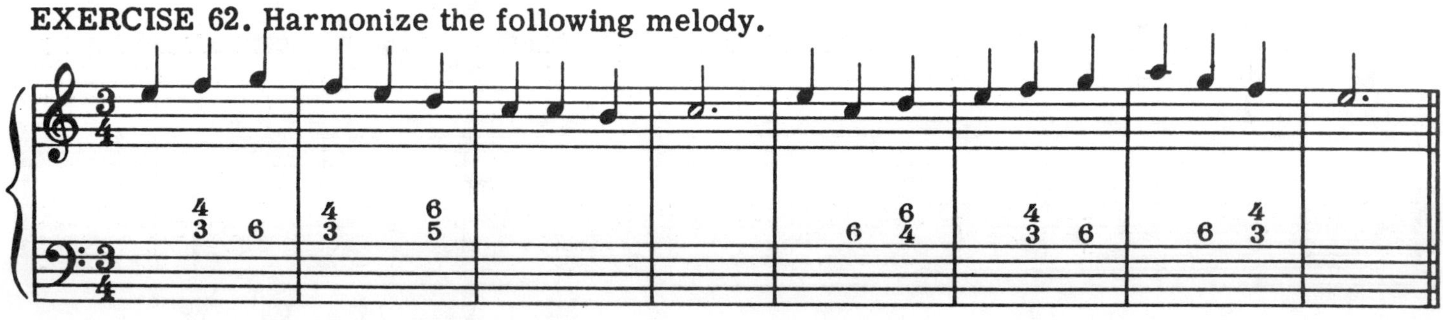

EXERCISE 63. Harmonize the following melody.

CHAPTER 11
Minor Triads

Minor Triads occur on the second, II, third, III, and sixth, VI, degrees of the major scale. They are composed of a root, a minor third and a perfect fifth.

VARIOUS POSITIONS OF THE MINOR TRIADS OF C

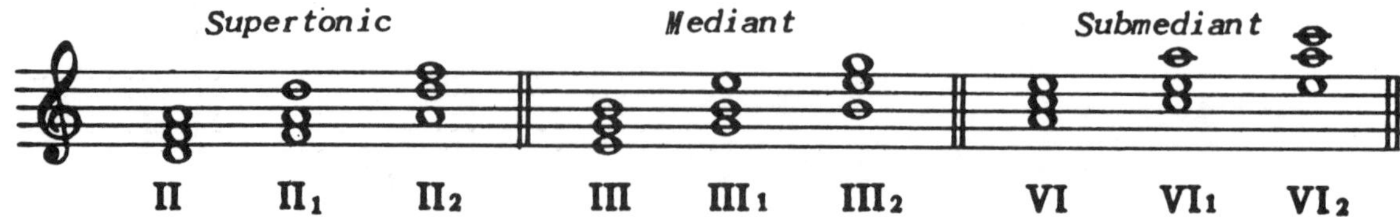

The Supertonic, II, may follow the Tonic, I, or the Subdominant, IV. Sing these progressions. Name the chords as they are played.

The Submediant, VI, may follow the Tonic, I, or the Dominant Seventh, V7, Sing these progressions. Name the chords as they are played.

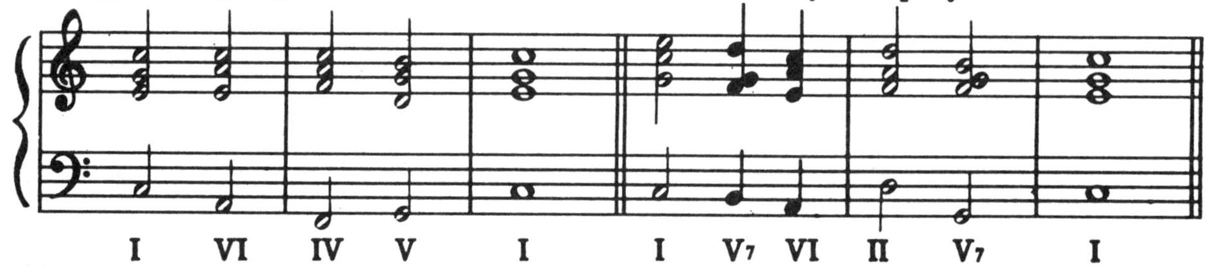

The Mediant, III, may follow the Tonic, I; or the Dominant, V. Sing these progressions. Name the chords as they are played.

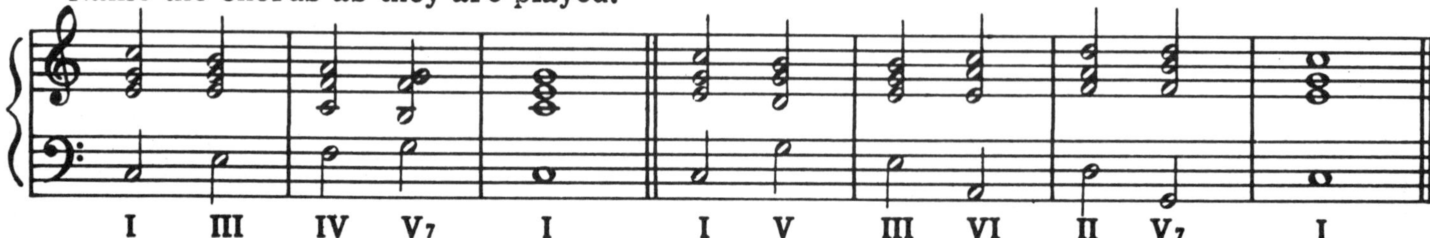

EXERCISE 64. Fill in the two lower treble parts.

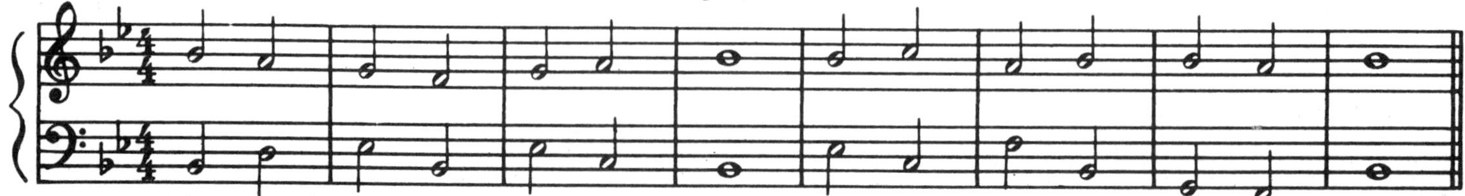

EXERCISE 65. Fill in the two lower treble parts.

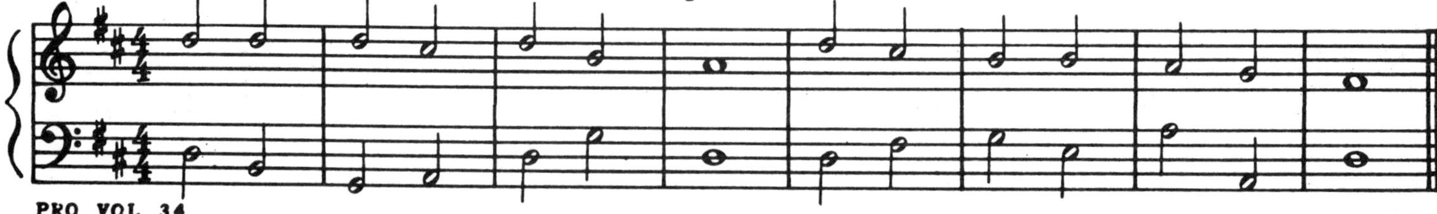

EXERCISE 66. Harmonize the following melody.

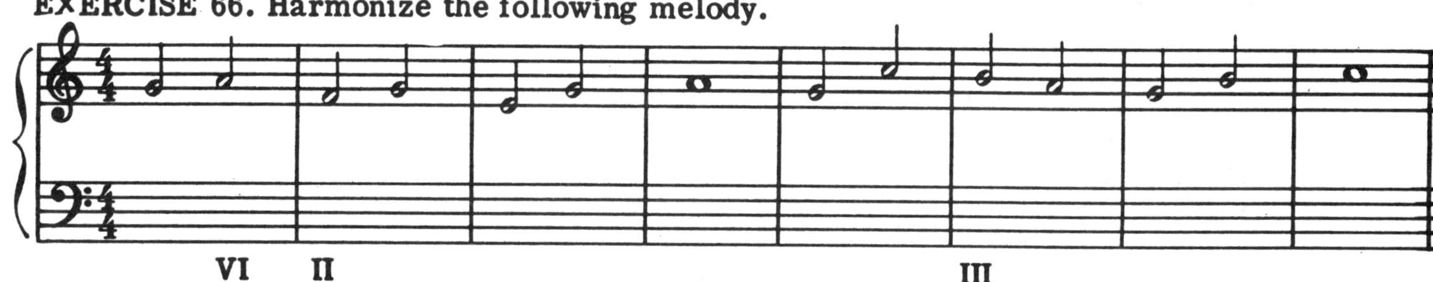

EXERCISE 67. Harmonize the following melody.

Inversions of the Minor Triads are figured the same as Major Triads. In the 1st inversion, unlike Major Triads, the third may be doubled in the upper voices.

II_6 or II_1 II^6_4 or II_2 III_6 or III_1 III^6_4 or III_2 VI_6 or VI_1 VI^6_4 or VI_2

EXERCISE 68. Fill in the two lower treble parts.

EXERCISE 69. Fill in the two lower treble parts.

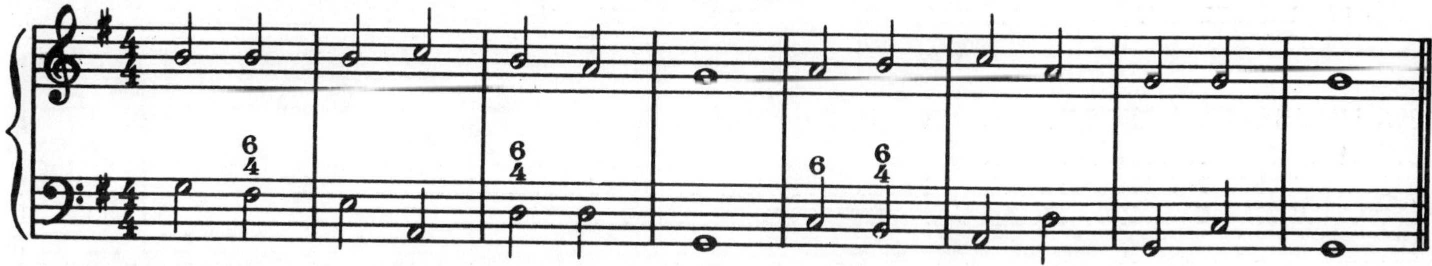

EXERCISE 70. Harmonize the following bass passage.

Although consecutive fifths and octaves are used in modern harmony, the student should avoid them until modern chord progressions have been studied. The following progressions are poor because of the two fifths following each other.

Sing these progressions. Note the consecutive fifths.

The same chord progressions will sound smoother this way.

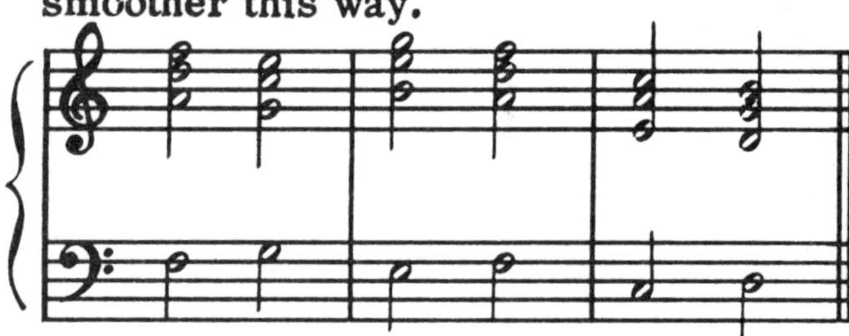

EXERCISE 71. Harmonize the following bass passages so that there will be no consecutive fifths. Use 1st inversions where possible. Write the soprano first then fill in the chords you will use.

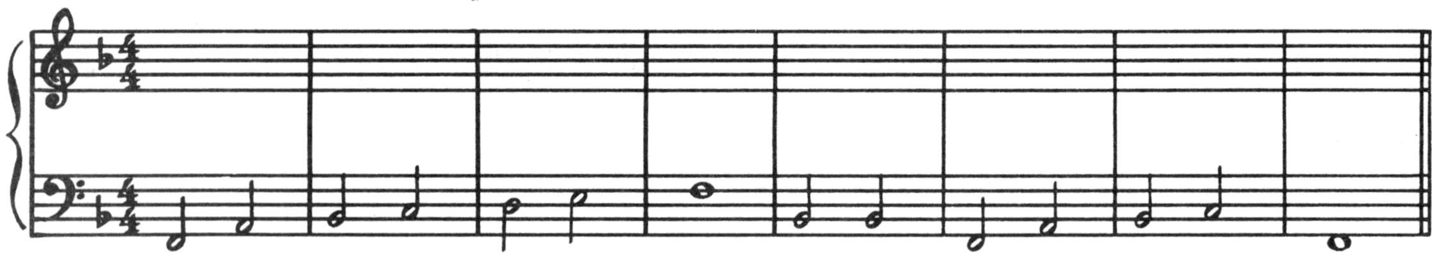

EXERCISE 72. Harmonize the following melody.

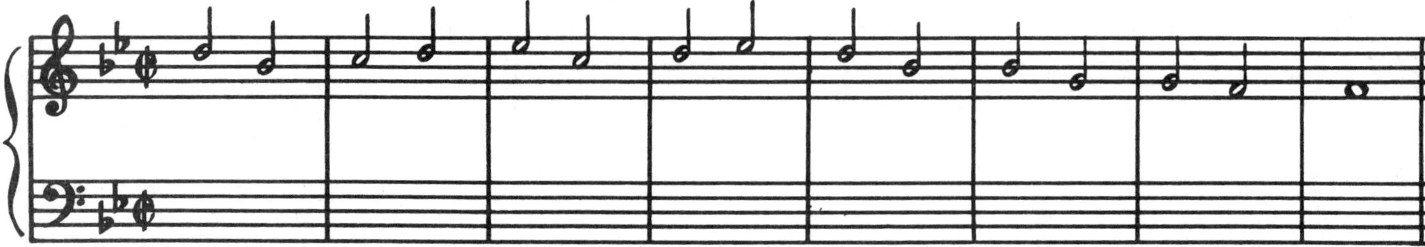

CHAPTER 12
Non-Harmonic or Passing Tones

All melodies harmonized so far have consisted only of chord tones. A good many melodies contain tones which do not belong to the chords with which they sound. These tones are called Non-harmonic or Passing. They either move too fast to be harmonized separately or the writer does not wish to use the more complex harmony they would require. The most common occurrence is in a fast moving melody with a harmonic background. In the following examples the passing tones are marked with an X.

IRISH WASHERWOMAN

Another example of passing tones is the melody with a rhythmic background.

YANKEE DOODLE

Here is the same melody in four part harmony.

EXERCISE 73. First mark the passing tones in the following, then arrange in four part harmony, as in the preceding example.
The B♭ in the third measure is not a passing tone. Can you tell why?

LONDON BRIDGE

EXERCISE 74. Mark the passing tones in the following melodies.

TURKEY IN THE STRAW

SAILOR'S HORNPIPE

CHAPTER 13
Two and Three Part Harmony

In three part harmony, the bass is omitted. Tones are seldom doubled. All the tones of a triad usually appear. The root or fifth of a dominant seventh is omitted.

In two part harmony. intervals of a third, sixth, diminished fifth and augmented fourth, sound best. Perfect fourths and fifths should be avoided, as they sound hollow and incomplete. The third of each chord is nearly always present.

Compare the following two and three part arrangements of the same melody. Sometimes the middle and sometimes the low voice of a trio arrangement is better for a duet- But seldom is either used in its entirety. Sing these harmonizations.

MY MARYLAND

In two part harmony, sometimes both parts will have passing or non-harmonic notes. In the first example the passing tones are marked. Try to find them yourself in the second example.

BLUE BELLS OF SCOTLAND

LA PALOMA

EXERCISE 75. First fill in the duet harmony on the first staff. Then fill in the third part on the second staff. Why do we double the melody note here*? Sing what you have written to be sure you are following the rules set forth previously.

WHISPERING HOPE

Sometimes when a melody makes a high skip, it is expedient to use open harmony. In a close arrangement, the harmony notes may be too high for the instruments for which they are intended, or the progression may be bad, such as the two fifths following each other in the first example below. Sing both arrangements so that you hear the difference.

OLD FOLKS AT HOME

EXERCISE 76. Fill in duet part, third part and piano accompaniment. Try to sing the root of each chord you will use before filling in the chords to establish the chord feeling.

JUANITA

Three part harmony may be arranged two ways.

(1) With the duet part written first and the third part filled in afterward. This is called commercial arranging, as it can be used for either two or three instruments.

(2) In parallel harmony, This is smoother, but it can be used only as a trio. Sing these progressions and listen to the difference.

EXERCISE 77. Fill in duet part and third part. Use parallel harmony in the second strain.

TRAMP, TRAMP, TRAMP

CHAPTER 14
Minor Scales

The Relative Minor scale begins on the sixth degree of the Major scale, and has the same key signature. In the Pure or Natural form it consists of the same tones as the Major.

EXERCISE 78. Name the Relative Minor of 10 other Major scales.

1.......... 3.......... 5.......... 7.......... 9..........

2.......... 4.......... 6.......... 8.......... 10..........

EXERCISE 79. Write the Pure Minor scale on each of the Keynotes G D F B♭ with their proper key signatures.

In the Harmonic form the seventh or leading tone of the Pure Minor is raised a half step by an accidental which does not appear in the signature.

Sing all of these scales to hear the difference in tonality between major and minor and the modality between the two minor scales.

EXERCISE 80. Write the Harmonic Minor scale on each of the keynotes C F G D.

The Minor scale that begins on the same keynote as a Major scale is called its Tonic Minor. Therefore A Minor is the Tonic Minor of A Major as well as the Relative Minor of C Major. To summarize: The Relative Minor has the same key signature as the Major and the Tonic Minor has the same keynote as the Major.

In the Melodic form, both sixth and seventh tones of the Pure or Natural minor scale are raised a half step ascending, but the scale descends in the Pure form.

EXERCISE 81. Write the three forms of the minor scale on the keynote E.

EXERCISE 82. Below are two well known melodies written in the minor. State which is Harmonic and which is Melodic and why.

a)

b)

EXERCISE 83. Write the following major melodies in the Tonic Minor, using the Harmonic form.

EXERCISE 84. Write the following major melodies in the Tonic Minor, using the Melodic form.

CHAPTER 15

Modern Chord Names and Symbols

Figured Bass, although an excellent study to develop the use of smooth flowing bass passages, is inadequate to express the complex chords of modern harmony. Today we have a system, born of necessity, whereby every chord is named by its root, regardless of key. This system is clear, concise and efficient. There can be only one name for a chord, no matter in what key it appears. Under the old system a chord will have a different name in every key.

Take for instance our old friend the major triad on C. In the key of C, if the Tonic is in the bass, it would be I. With the third in the bass, I_6. With the fifth in the bass, I^6_4. In the key of G, it would be IV, IV_6 or IV^6_4. In the key of F, it would be V, V_6 or V^6_4.

The Dominant Seventh chord is called V_7, which means nothing without knowing the Tonic. In the modern system the chord is a G seventh in any key or in any position or inversion. The chord is simply D minor in any key, instead of being II in the key of C, III in the key of B♭ and VI in the key of F.

All the major, minor and seventh chords are now shown in the order of their normal root progressions, from C to C through the cycle of fifths. In the enharmonic change from G♭ to F♯, chords are raised an octave so that the treble clef may be used throughout.

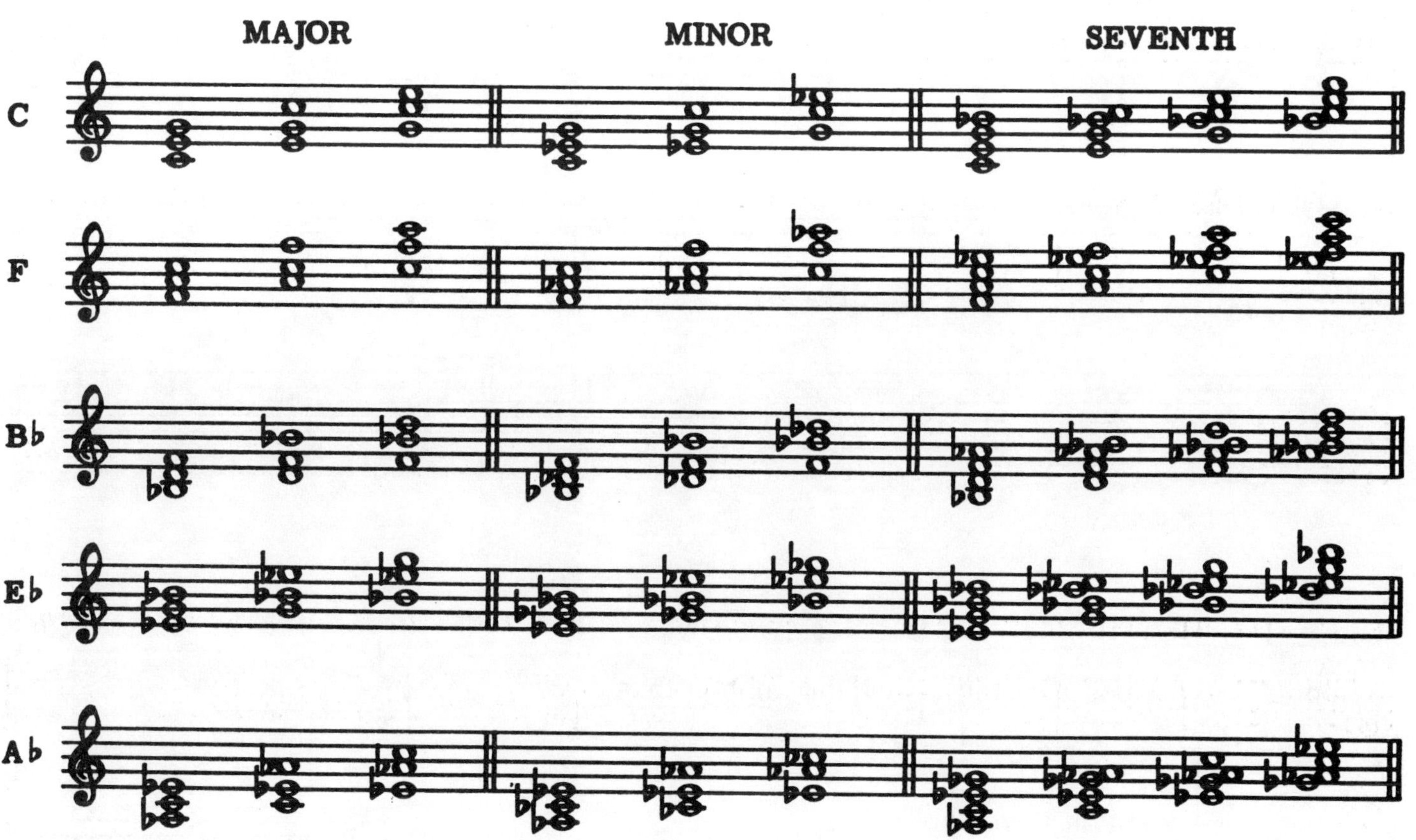

Major Minor Seventh

D♭

G♭

F♯

B

E

A

D

G

C

Symbols are placed over the chord and appear thus:

Major Triad - C or CM
Minor Triad - Cm or Cmi
Dominant Seventh - C7

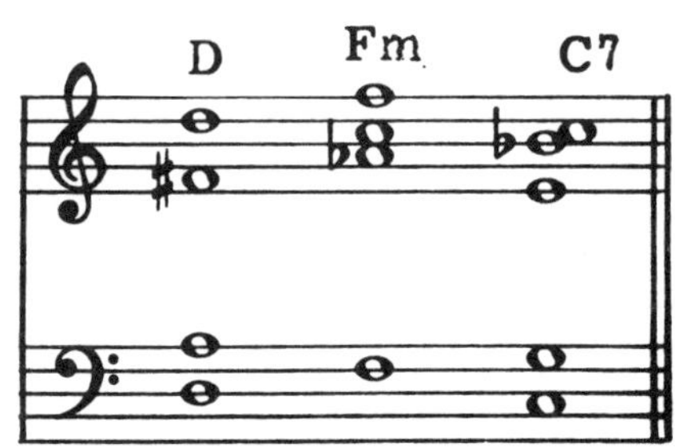

EXERCISE 85. Place the symbol over each of the following chords.

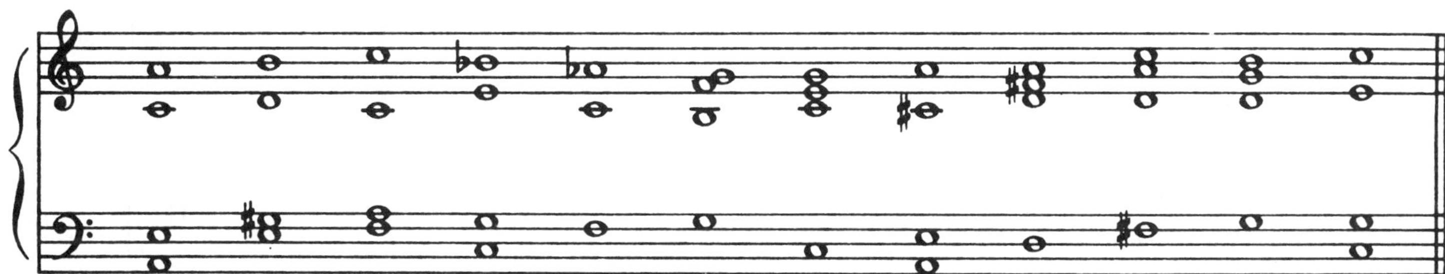

EXERCISE 86. Place the symbols over the chords in the following excerpt. Mark the passing tones in both clefs with an X.

SARABANDE

Handel

EXERCISE 87. Place the symbols over the chords in the following excerpts. In No.2 the bass note must be considered with the following chord. Mark the passing tone with an X. The chord marked* has not yet been studied.

CHAPTER 16
Chord Root Progressions

A chord may progress to another chord whose root is either a perfect fourth above or a perfect fifth below. The diminished triad, **VII,** is seldom used as a fundamental chord, so we show a minor triad on the seventh degree. In modern harmony, the VII chord is treated as a V_7 chord, with the root missing.

Sing these progressions. Try to name the chords as you hear them.

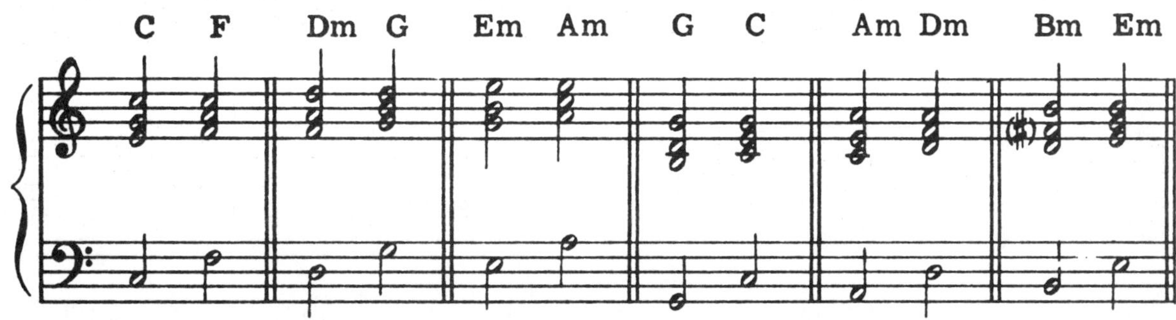

Showing other progressions on the same roots. Either major, minor or seventh chords may be used.

The progression of chord roots through the cycle of fifths is called Normal or Harmonic. It is often found in a series or sequential pattern.

EXERCISE 88. Harmonize each pair of chord roots in a different way.

Showing the progression of dominant sevenths through the cycle of fifths.

EXERCISE 89. Harmonize the same chord roots with alternate major and minor chords. Be careful to get in all the accidentals.

A chord may progress to another chord whose root is either a perfect fifth above or a perfect fourth below. In this case also, we show a minor triad instead of the diminished triad, VII. Sing these progressions.

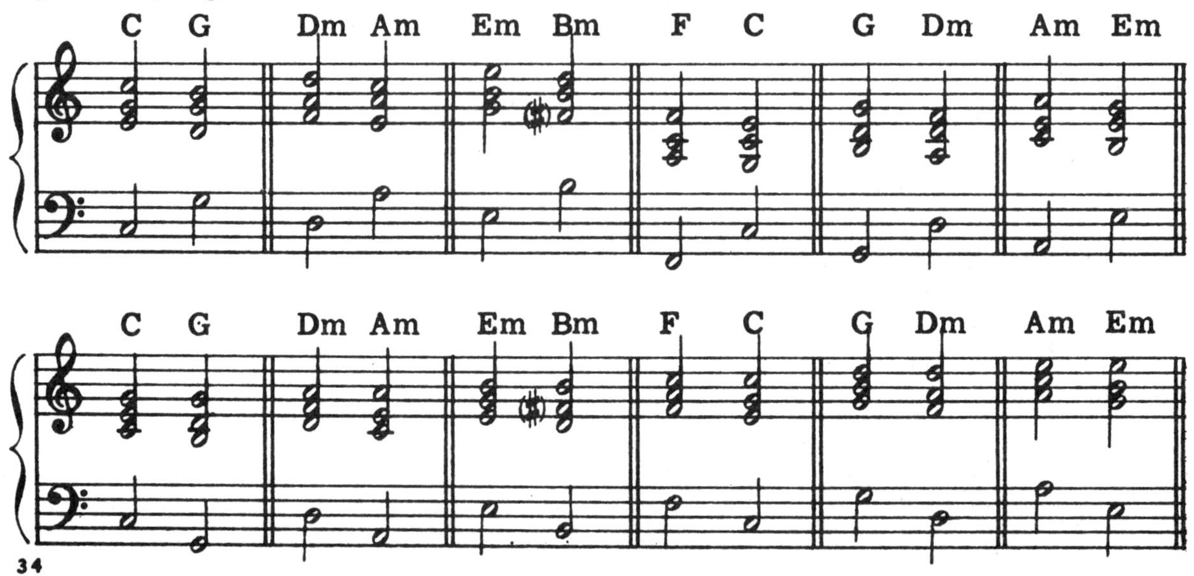

As this progression usually involves the dominant, the tendency is to return to the tonic. Unlike our first set of chord roots, it is never found in a series.

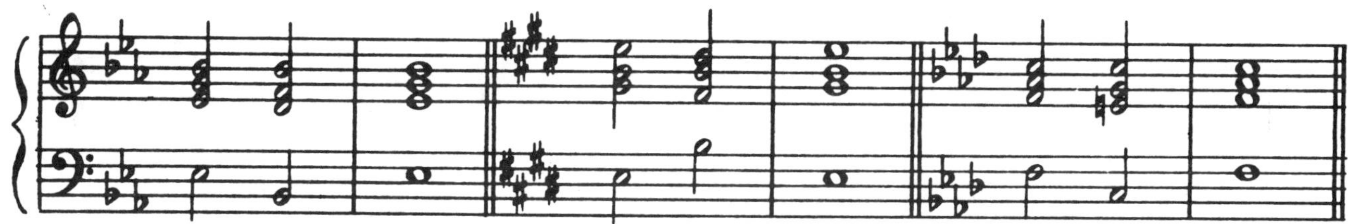

All major, minor or seventh chords built on degrees of a major scale are relative to its key.

EXERCISE 90. Write all the chords relative to the key of B♭.

A chord may progress to another chord whose root is either a major or minor third above. First we show progressions to chords on the degrees of the major scale. These progressions are common as they are relative to the scale. Sing these progressions, then name the chords as they are played. These progressions of rising thirds are used in passages that are rhythmically unaccented.

Now we show progressions to chords on degrees which are foreign to the scale. These progressions are not so common.

A chord may progress to another chord whose root is either a major or minor third below. First we have the common progressions to chords on the degrees of the major scale. These progressions of falling thirds are again rhythmically unaccented.

Now we have progressions to chords on degrees foreign to the scale.

So far we have shown that any major, minor or seventh chord may progress to any other major, minor or seventh chord whose root is:

- A perfect fourth above or below.
- A perfect fifth above or below.
- A major third above or below.
- A minor third above or below.

EXERCISE 91. Fill in the two lower treble parts. Place the symbol over each chord. Remember that the root is not always in the bass.

An accidental in the melody sometimes indicates the third of a new chord. It is usually better to have contrary motion between the bass and melody. This sometimes calls for an inverted chord.

EXERCISE 92. Harmonize the following melodies.

Progression is often extended by the use of two different chords in succession on the same root. Sing these progressions. Name the chords as they are played.

EXERCISE 93. Fill in the two lower treble parts.

A chord may progress to another chord whose root is either a major or minor second above: When the root interval is a minor second, the chord progression is usually chromatic, each note a half step higher.

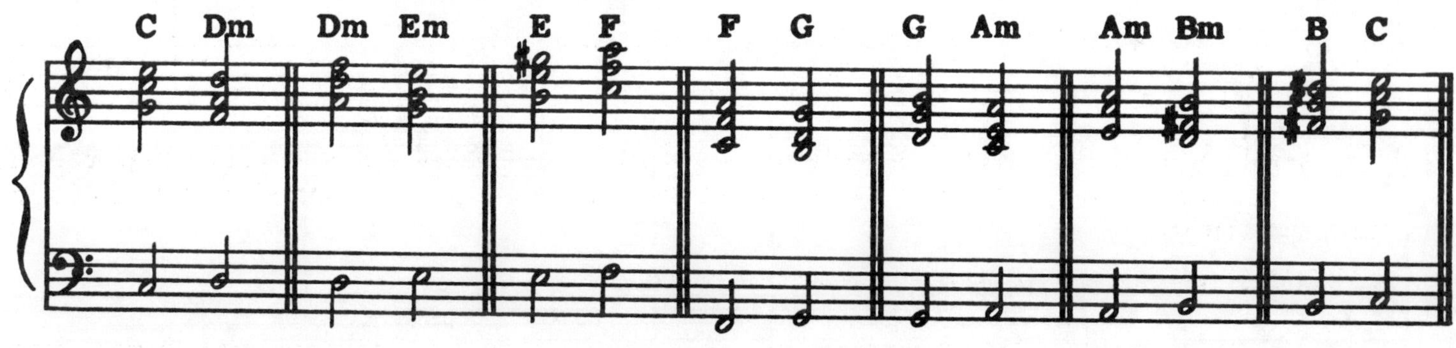

A chord may progress to another chord whose root is either a major or minor second below. As before, when the root interval is a minor second, the chord progression is usually chromatic, each note a half step lower. The minor second is sometimes written as an augmented prime, with the whole chord changed enharmonically. Sing these progressions. Name the chords as they are played.

This progression is often disguised by using inverted chords.

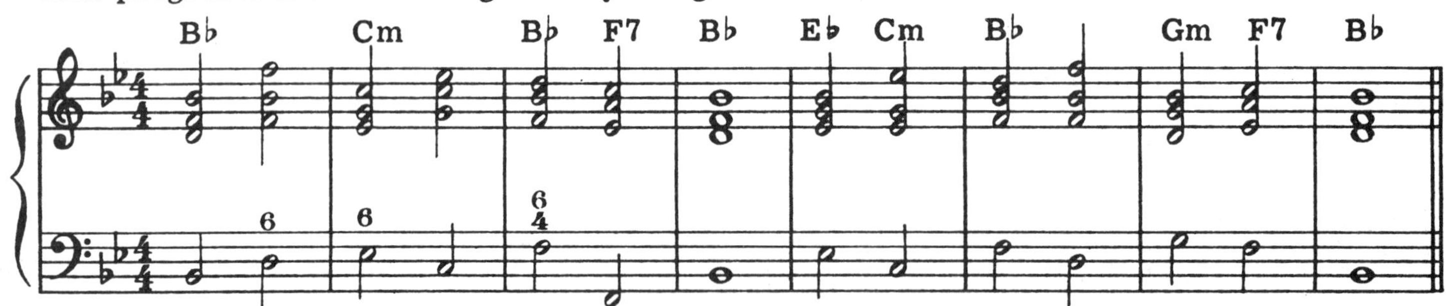

The chromatic chord progression is also disguised by inversion.

In harmonizing a melody, it should always be kept in mind that we must finish with some form of the tonic chord. It would be wise for the student at this point to stick to chords which are relative to the key. In doing so, we are on the main track (the cycle of fifths) back to the tonic chord.

EXERCISE 94. Fill in the two lower treble parts.

EXERCISE 95. Fill in the two lower treble parts. Watch out for passing tones.

EXERCISE 96. Harmonize the following melodies. Watch out for passing tones.

CHAPTER 17
The Minor Seventh Chord

The Minor Seventh chord is formed by adding the minor seventh interval to the minor triad. It is composed of a root, a minor third, a perfect fifth, and a minor seventh. The symbol is Am7 or Ami7.

It will be noticed that this chord contains both a major triad and its relative minor triad: as in the above example, a major triad on C, and a minor triad on A. This chord may be used in place of either triad it contains.

In the original position, with the root in the bass, it is predominantly minor.

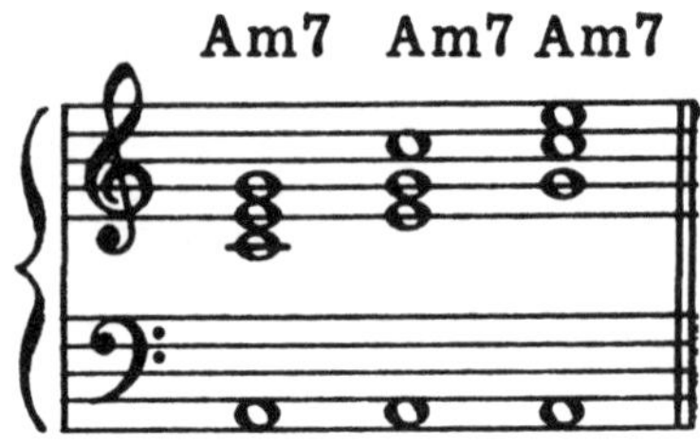

In the 1st inversion, with the 3rd in the bass, it becomes major in quality, and is sometimes called a Major Sixth, with the 3rd considered as the root.

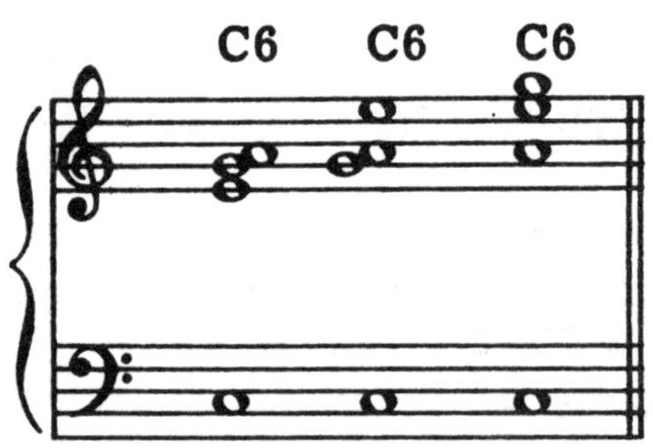

In the 2nd and 3rd inversions, it retains its minor quality.

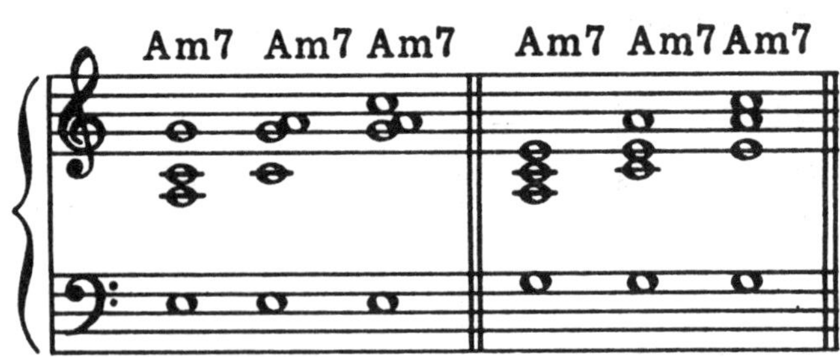

EXERCISE 97. Fill in the two lower treble parts.

EXERCISE 98. Fill in the two lower treble parts.

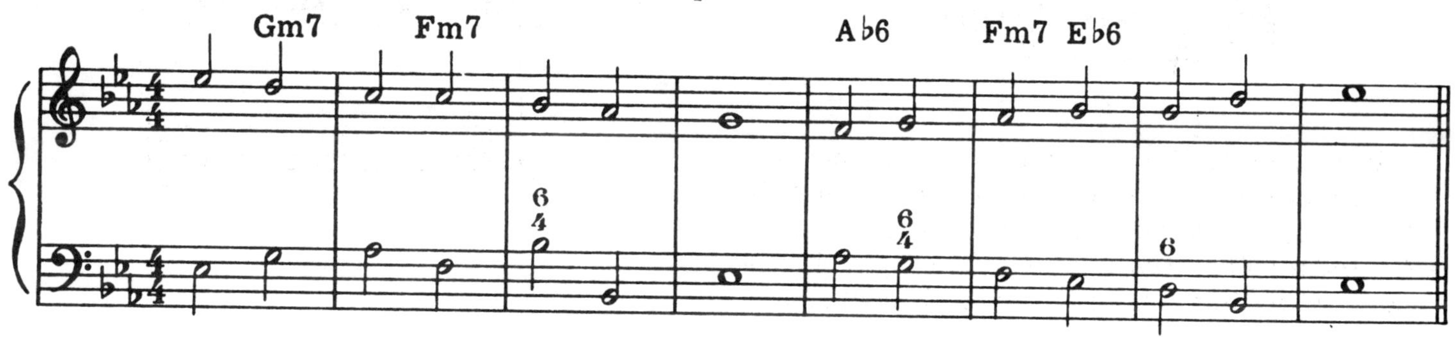

EXERCISE 99. Harmonize the following bass passage.

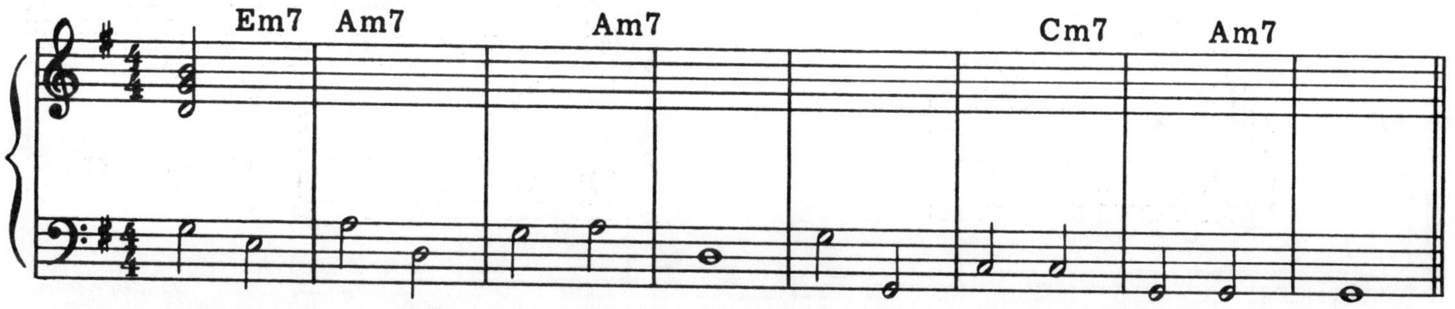

EXERCISE 100. Harmonize the following melody.

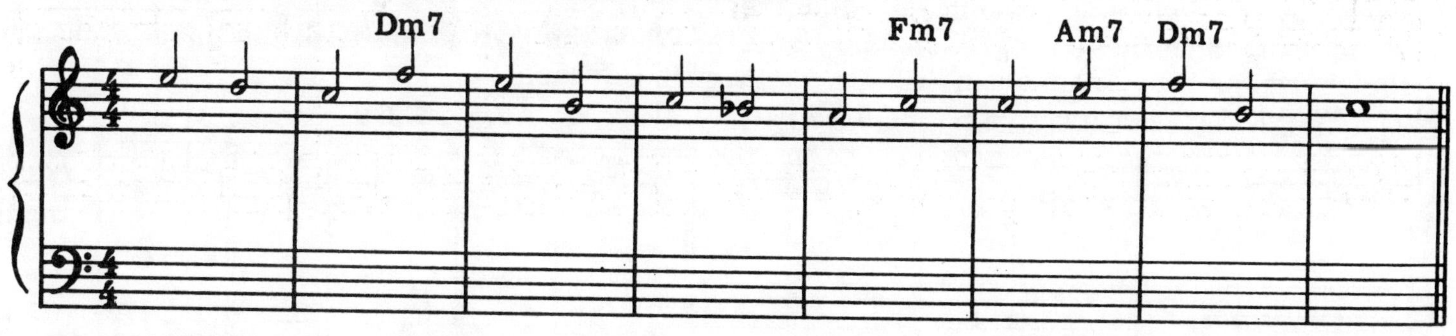

CHAPTER 18

The Dominant Ninth Chord

The Dominant Ninth chord is formed by adding the major ninth interval to the dominant seventh chord. It has the same inversions as the dominant seventh, and may be used instead. In four part harmony, the root, third or fifth is omitted. The ninth is usually found in the top voice, rarely the root. The symbol is G9.

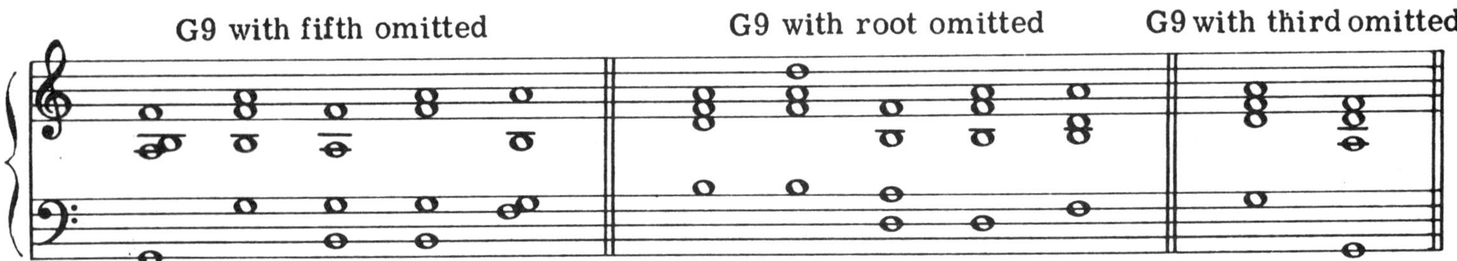

In the second inversion, with the root omitted, this chord has a minor quality, and is sometimes called a Minor Sixth, with the fifth considered as the root and usually doubled.

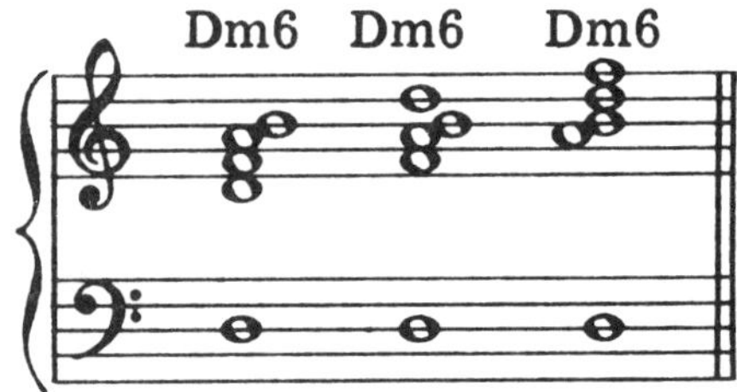

In four part harmony, the fifth is most often omitted.

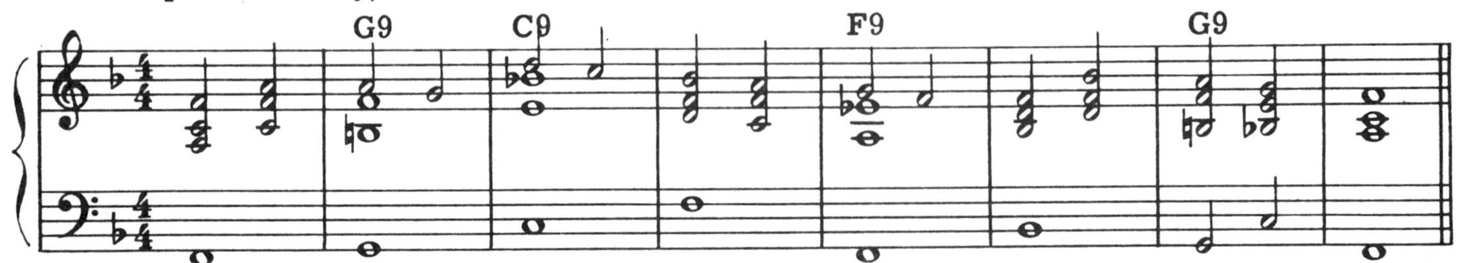

The third is sometimes omitted when followed by the dominant seventh chord on the same root. Sing these progressions. Name the chords as they are played.

When the root is omitted, the third is usually in the bass.

EXERCISE 101. Fill in the two lower treble parts.

EXERCISE 102. Fill in the two lower treble parts.

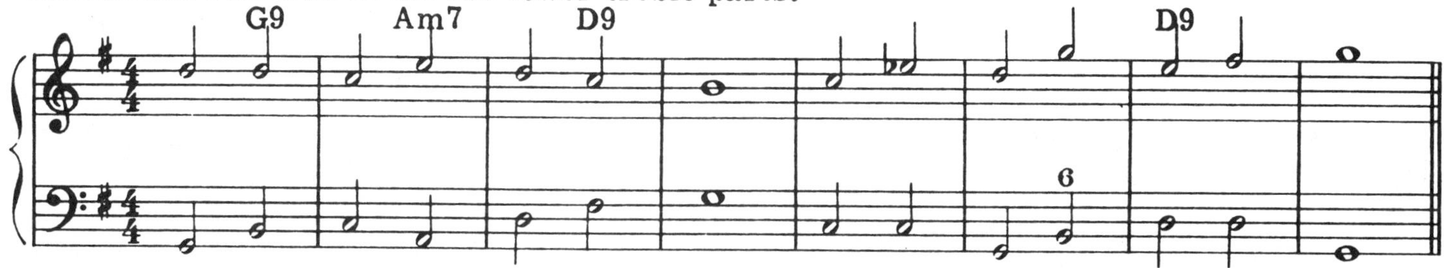

The Dominant Ninth chord is sometimes found in a chromatic series. This is one case where consecutive fifths are permissible.

The discrimination between a dominant ninth with a root omitted, and a minor sixth, depends on the resolution. All dominant chords resolve naturally to the tonic. In the first example following, the chord root progression B♭ to E♭ is dominant to tonic, so we call the chord a dominant ninth. In the second example, as the chord root progression B♭ to C would not be dominant to tonic, we consider the fifth as the root and call the chord a minor sixth. This chord usually progresses to a 2nd inversion.

EXERCISE 103. Fill in the two lower treble parts.

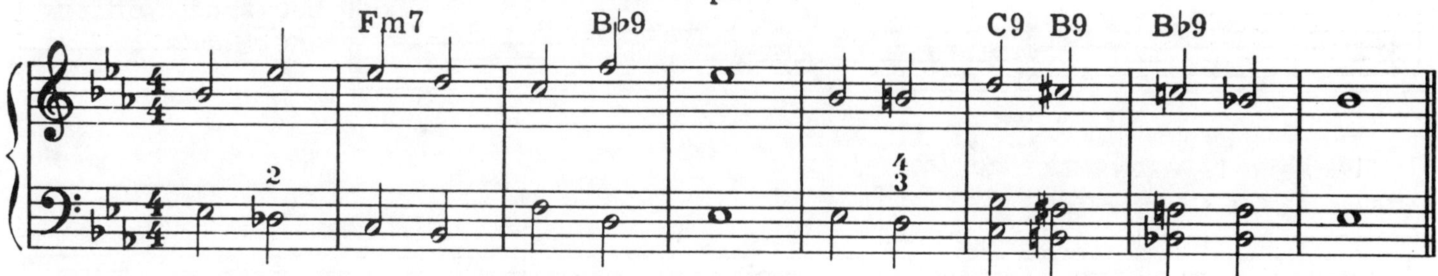

EXERCISE 104. Harmonize the following melody.

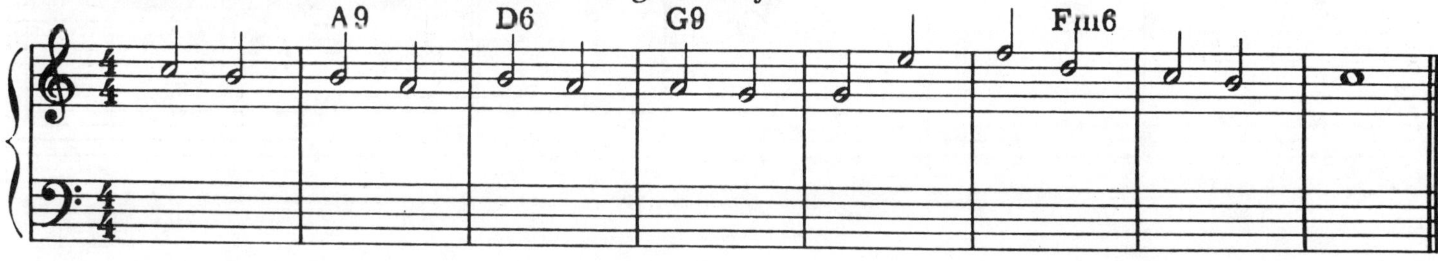

CHAPTER 19
The Diminished Seventh Chord

The Diminished Seventh chord is composed of a root, a minor third, a diminished fifth and a diminished seventh. The symbol is C dim. or C dim. 7.

Correct notation of a Diminished Seventh on C.

As the correct notation is often hard to read, enharmonic equivalents are used.

In close harmony the tones of a Diminished Seventh chord are an equal distance (minor third) apart.

Enharmonically, there are only three of these chords, since if we continue ascending chromatically, we keep repeating the first three chords. Therefore any note of the chord may be considered as the root. The Diminished Seventh chord can usually be distinquished by two accidentals.

This chord may be used as a bridge between two similar chords. Sing these progressions.

Or it may be used as a transitional or passing chord between two different chords.

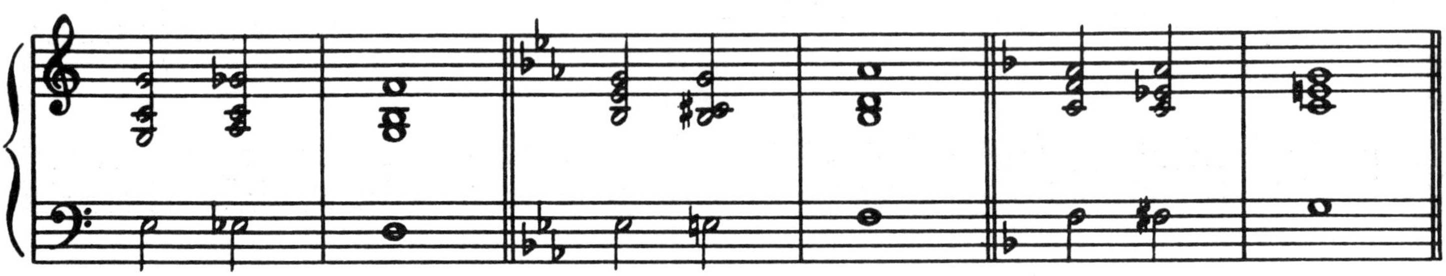

Each tone of a Diminished Seventh chord must resolve to the nearest tone of the next chord. Sing these progressions.

EXERCISE 105. Fill in the two lower treble parts.

EXERCISE 106. Fill in the two lower treble parts.

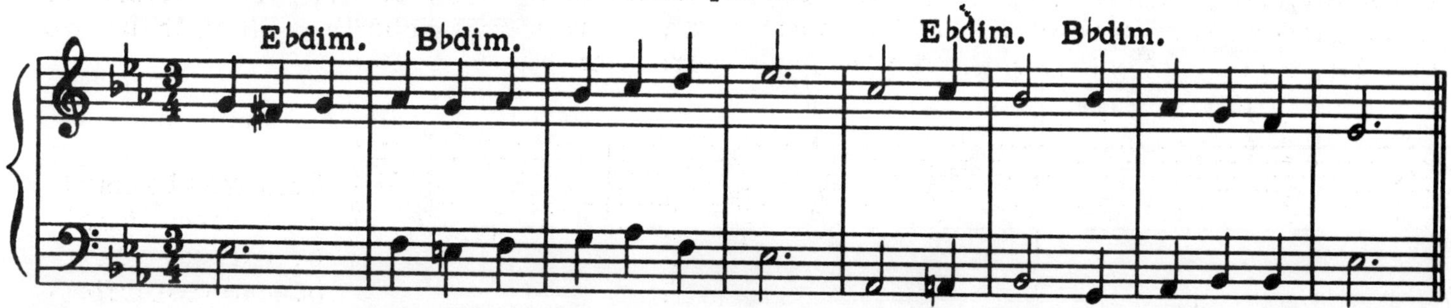

EXERCISE 107. Harmonize the following bass passage.

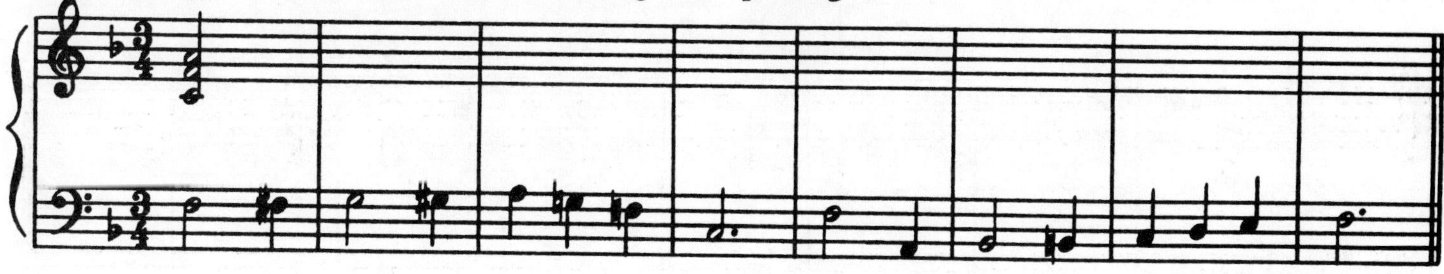

CHAPTER 20
The Augmented Fifth Chord

The Augmented Fifth chord is composed of a root, a major third and an augmented fifth. It resolves to the major or minor triad of which its root is the dominant. It may displace either the dominant seventh or ninth chord. The symbol is C aug. C + 5 or C +.

In close harmony, the tones of an Augmented Fifth chord are an equal distance (2 tones) apart.

Enharmonically, there are only four of these chords, since if we continue ascending chromatically, we keep repeating the first four chords. Therefor any note of the chord could be the root. But care should be taken to use the correct notation.

For instance, when C is the third, A♭ would be the root, not G♯.

A♭ aug.

or when F is the root, C♯ would be the fifth, not D♭.

F aug.

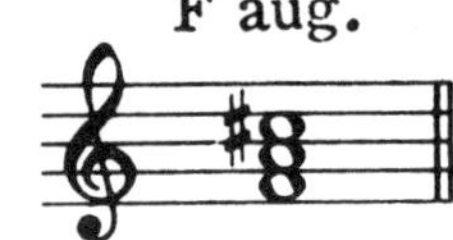

In four part harmony, the root is usually doubled, occasionally the third, but seldom the fifth.

Occasionally the Augmented Fifth chord will resolve to a dominant seventh or ninth of which its root is the dominant. In the case of the D aug. chord below, the augmented fifth interval appears enharmonically as B♭. Sing this progression.

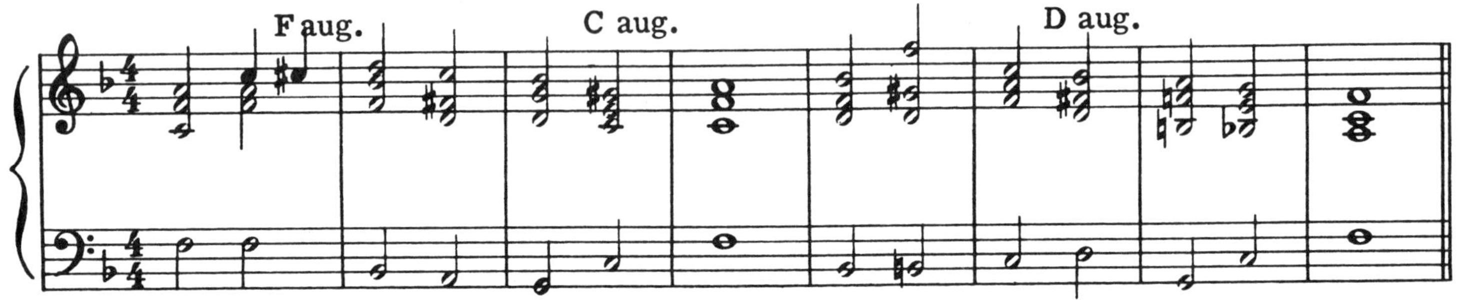

EXERCISE 108. Fill in the two lower treble parts.

EXERCISE 109. Harmonize the following melody.

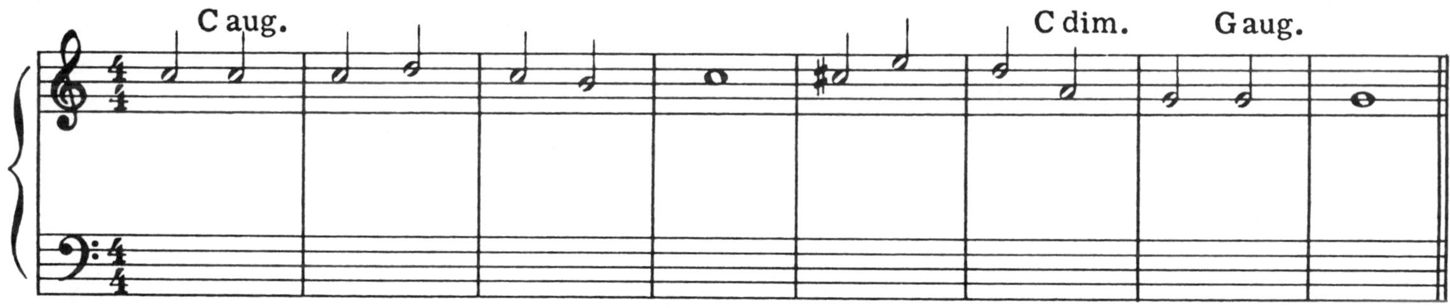

EXERCISE 110. Fill in the two lower treble parts.

CHAPTER 21
Clefs and Transposition

All music writing today for orchestral and band instruments is done in one or more of the four clefs, namely, the G or treble clef, the F or bass clef, or either one of two C clefs, the alto and tenor. All of these clefs are derived from the Great Staff combining the treble and bass clefs with middle C between the two.

EXERCISE 111. Write in the pitch names of the great staff.

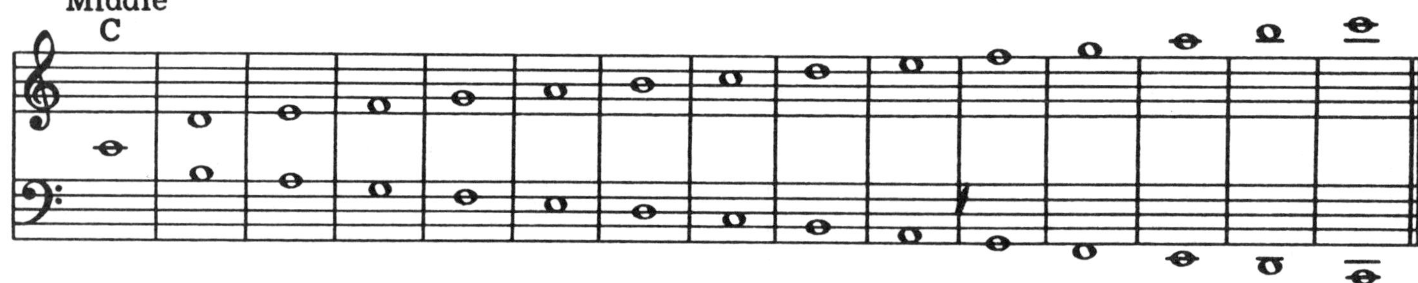

The alto clef, sometimes called the viola clef, is derived from the Great Staff by taking the two lower lines of the G clef, middle "C", and the two upper lines of the bass staff or F clef, then isolating this portion of the Great Staff on a staff of its own, as shown in the example which follows:

EXERCISE 112. Rewrite the pitches from treble clef into alto clef and name them.

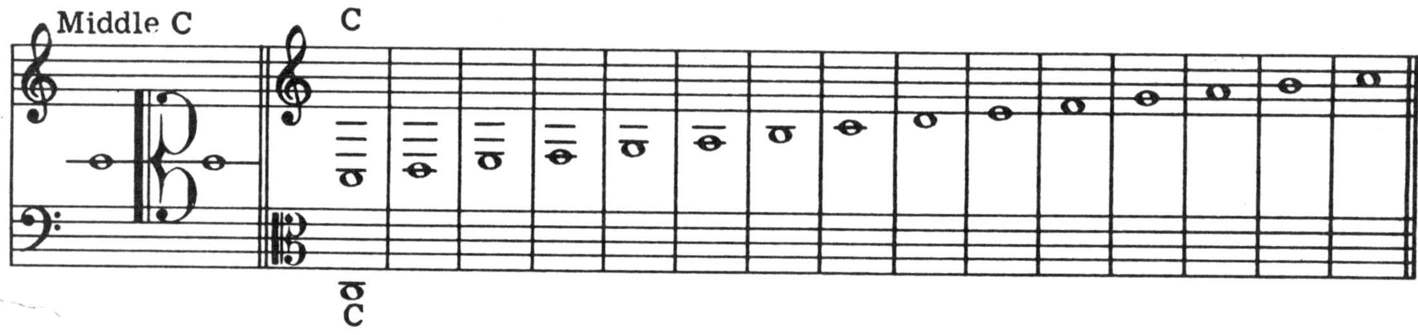

EXERCISE 113. Rewrite the following melody into alto clef.

Auld Lang Syne
Scotch Melody

EXERCISE 114. Rewrite the following melody from alto clef into treble clef.

Austrian Hymn
Haydn

The tenor clef is derived from the Great Staff by borrowing the lowest line of the treble clef, middle C, and the three upper lines of the bass clef, then isolating this new clef onto a staff of its own. Note now that middle "C" has moved to the fourth line of the staff. It still sounds the same middle "C" as that pictured on the Great Staff. This clef is used by cello, string bass, trombone, bassoon, baritone horn, when the music to be performed would require too many leger lines in the bass clef, and, therefore, simplifies reading by placing it on the staff.

EXERCISE 115. Rewrite the pitches from bass clef into tenor clef and name them.

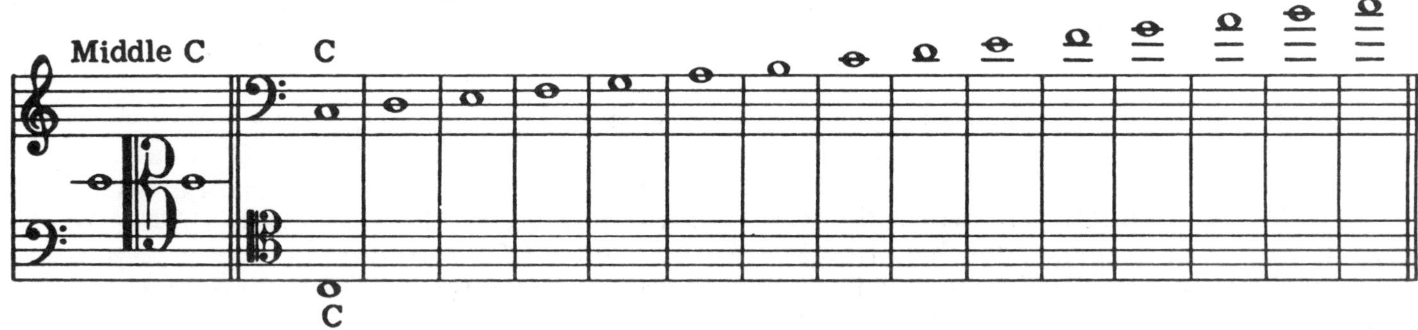

EXERCISE 116. Rewrite the following melody from bass clef into tenor clef.

Netherlands Hymn

EXERCISE 117. Rewrite the following melody from tenor into bass clef.

Silent Night
Franz Gruber

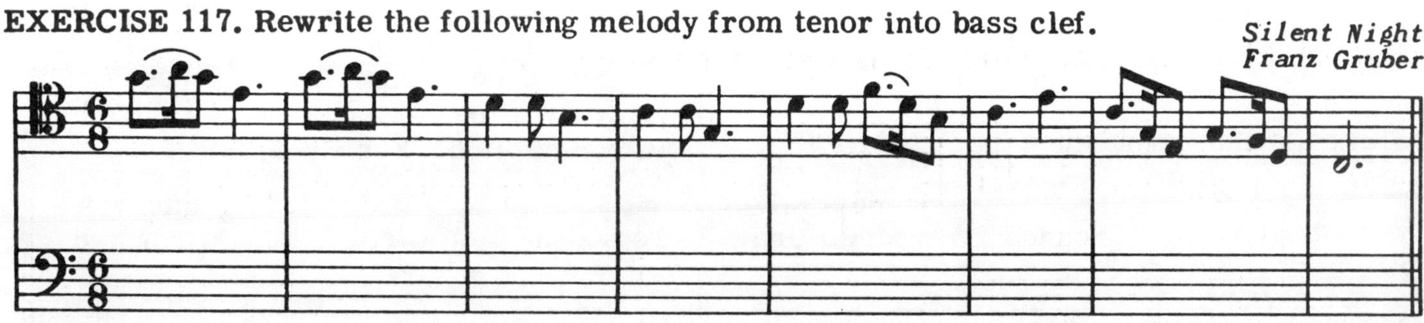

EXERCISE 118. Rewrite the following melody from alto into tenor clef.

Joy to the World
G. F. Handel

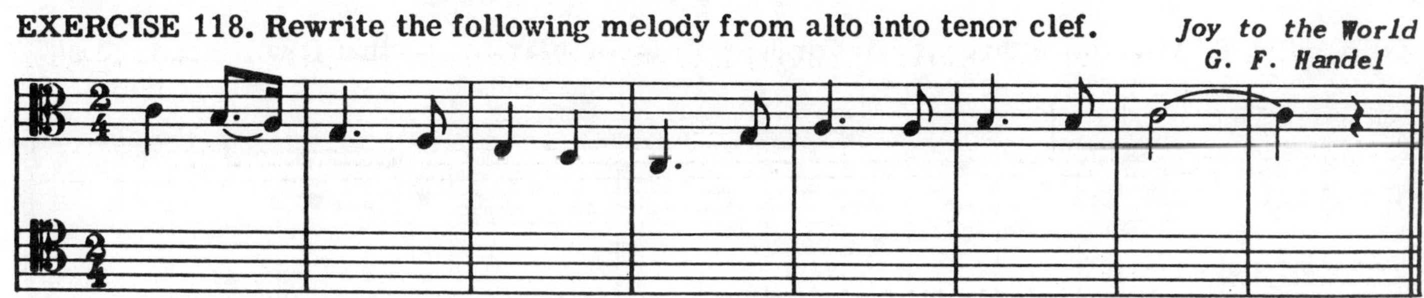

EXERCISE 119. Rewrite this duet into alto and tenor clefs.

TRANSPOSITION

The purpose of transposition is to enable a performer to use one system of fingering for a whole family of differently pitched instruments. Thus, in the saxophone family, we find saxophones built in C, B♭, E♭, F, BB♭, but when they read a "C" scale, they are all fingered alike, but sound different pitches with the same fingering.

For this reason, the composer and arranger must know transposition in order to make instruments, which sound pitches other than they read, be able to play together in unison and harmony. In this statement we find our definition of transposition.

A transposing instrument is one which sounds a pitch other than the one it reads, or, conversely, it reads pitches other than it sounds.

Instruments are labelled by their register, that is, sopranino, soprano, alto, tenor, baritone, bass, contra bass, and also by the pitch of the scale they sound when they read a "C" scale.

Thus, a B♭ instrument is one which sounds a B♭ scale when it reads a "C" scale. An E♭ instrument is one which sounds an E♭ scale when it reads "C" scale, etc.

The interval of transposition is measured on the Great Staff again from Middle "C". Sopranino transposing instruments all sound above Middle "C" when they read a "C" scale. Therefore, in order to be able to play in unison with the concert pitch, we must transpose, i.e. write, their music the same interval below Middle "C" that they sound above Middle "C". For example:

E♭ sopranino clarinets sound E♭, a minor third above middle "C" when reading the "C" scale. Therefore, all music for E♭ sopranino clarinets must be written a minor third below the concert pitch in order to sound in unison with the concert pitch. The transposed key, therefore, will be that found a minor third below Concert pitch. For example:

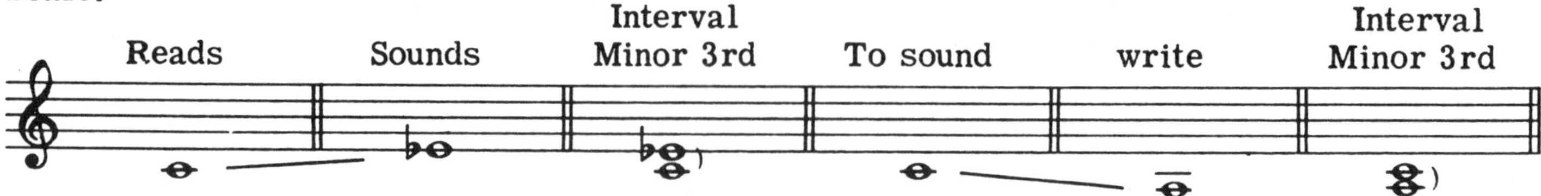

EXERCISE 120. Transpose this melody for E♭ sopranino clarinet so that it will sound in unison with concert pitch.

A D♭ Piccolo is a sopranino instrument which sounds a minor ninth above Concert Pitch, therefore, it must be written a minor ninth lower in order to sound in unison with concert pitch. See example below:

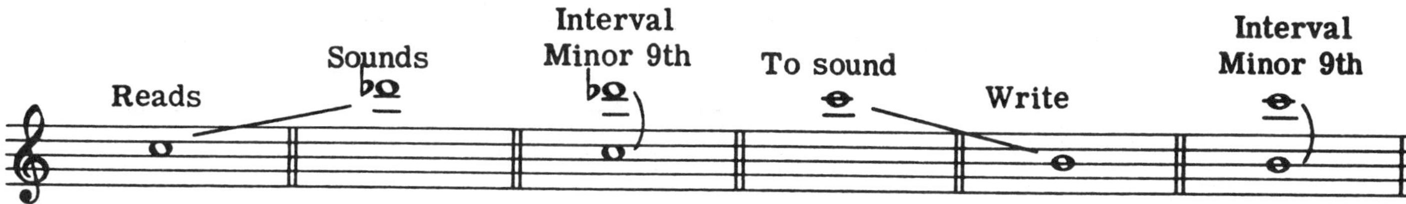

EXERCISE 121. Transpose this melody for D♭ Piccolo to sound in unison with concert pitch.

The B♭ Soprano instruments include clarinets, cornets, trumpets, saxophones. They sound a major second below "Middle C", so they must be written a major second above Middle "C". See example below:

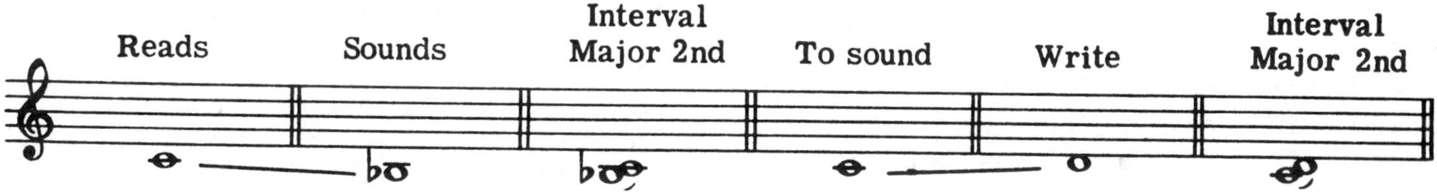

EXERCISE 122. Transpose this melody for B♭ soprano instruments to sound in unison with concert pitch.

The A soprano instruments include clarinets, cornets, trumpets, and sometimes, French Horns. They sound a minor third below concert pitch Middle "C", so they must be written a minor third above Middle "C". See example below:

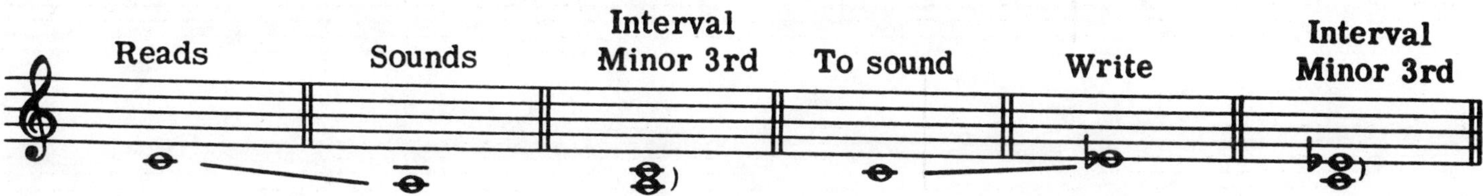

EXERCISE 123. Transpose this melody for A soprano instruments to sound in unison with concert pitch.

The G alto instruments include the Alto Flute, and sometimes French Horns. They sound a perfect fourth below concert pitch Middle "C", so they must be written a perfect fourth above concert pitch. See example below:

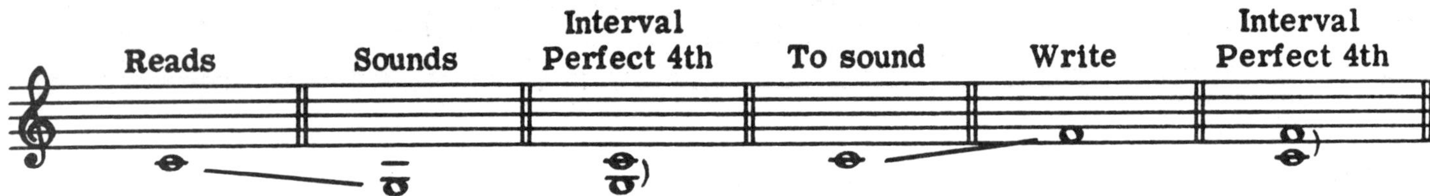

EXERCISE 124. Transpose this melody for G alto instruments to sound in unison with concert pitch.

The F alto instruments include the French Horn, English Horn, F Mezzo Saxophone, Mellophone and sometimes, Alto Horn. They sound a perfect fifth below concert pitch Middle "C", so they must be written a perfect fifth above concert pitch. See example below:

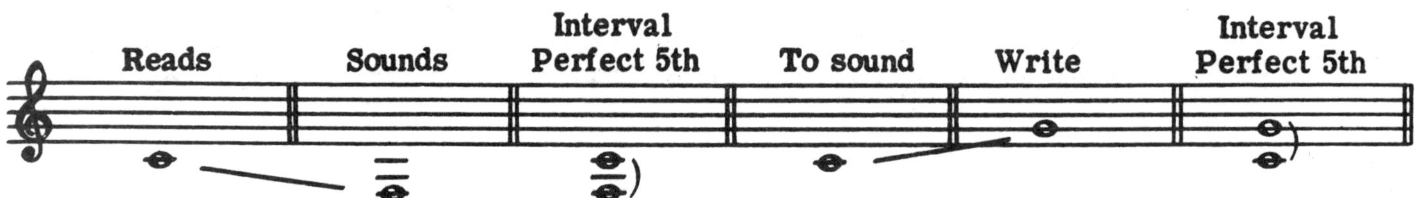

EXERCISE 125. Transpose this melody for F Alto instruments to sound in unison with concert pitch.

The E♭ Alto instruments include the Alto Saxophone, French Horns, Mellophones, Alto Horns. They sound a major sixth below concert pitch. See example below:

EXERCISE 126. Transpose this melody for E♭ Alto instruments to sound in unison with concert pitch.

The D alto instrument occasionally is the French Horn, which sounds a minor seventh below concert pitch Middle "C", and would, therefore, be written a minor seventh above concert pitch. See example below:

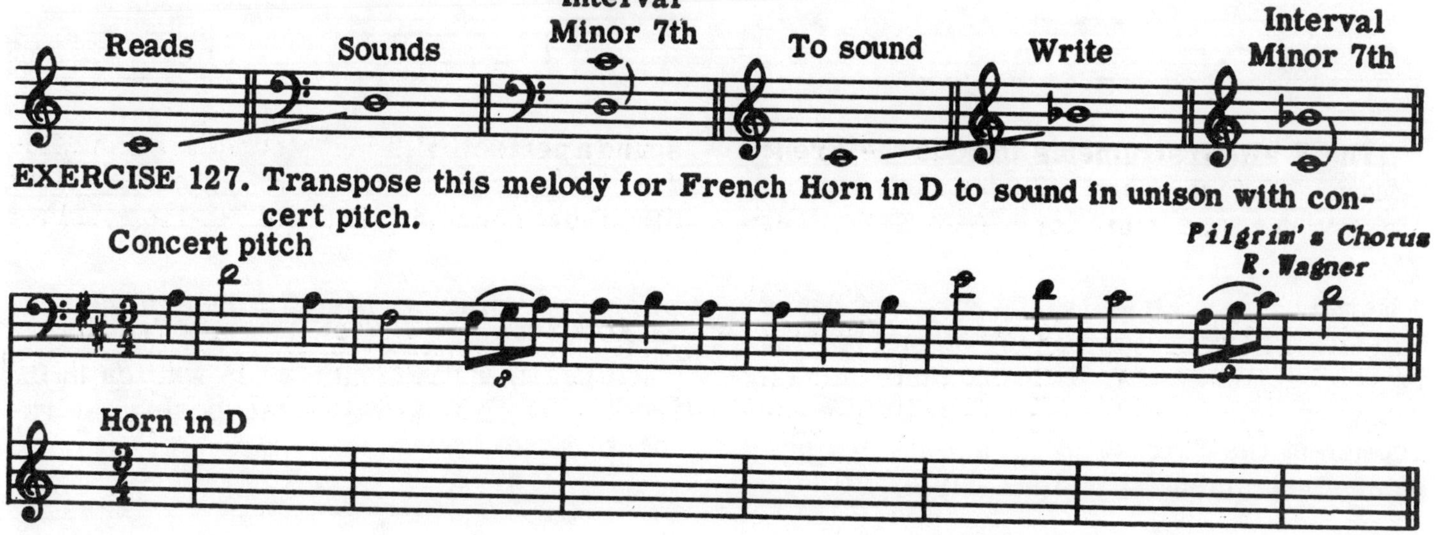

EXERCISE 127. Transpose this melody for French Horn in D to sound in unison with concert pitch.

The C tenor instruments include the C Melody Saxophone, the Bass Flute, The Haeckelphone, which is a baritone oboe sounding an octave lower than the Oboe. Parts for these instruments are simply written an octave higher than they actually sound, so there is no need to indicate any special transposition, but you must remember the actual sound they produce is lower than what is written.

There are also C contra-bass instruments written in the bass clef, the String Bass and the Contra-Bassoon, both of which sound an octave lower than they are reading. They are, therefore, transposing instruments.

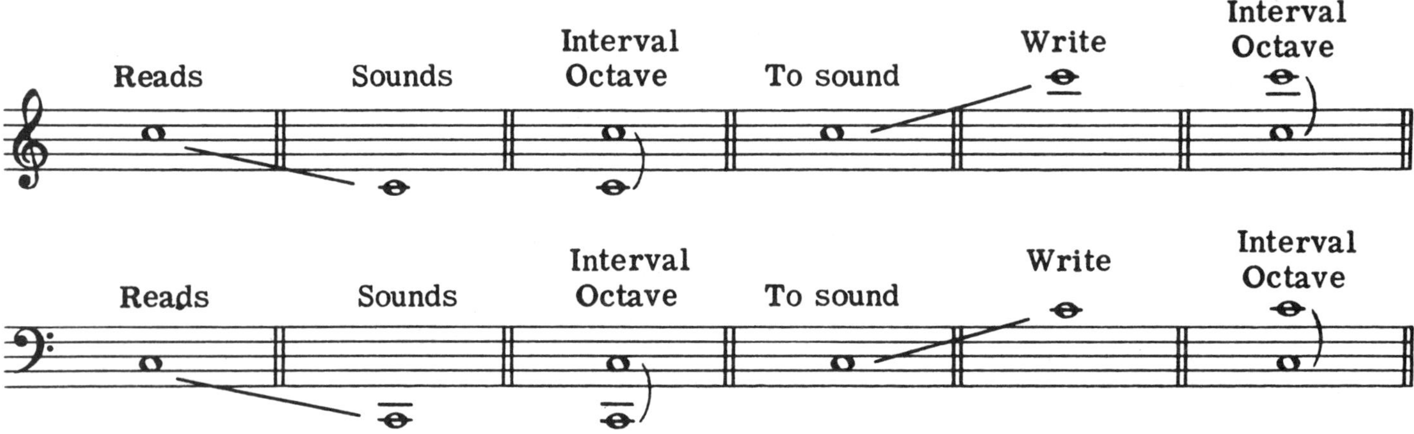

The B♭ tenor, baritone, and bass instruments, each with a different name, but all transposing the same interval include the B♭ Tenor Saxophone; the B♭ Bass Clarinet; the B♭ Baritone Horn; the B♭ Tenor Trombone; the B♭ Tenor Horn, all sound an octave and a major second, or rather, a major ninth below concert pitch Middle "C", and, therefore, must be written a major ninth above concert pitch. See example below:

EXERCISE 128. Transpose this melody for B♭ Tenor, Bass or Baritone instruments to sound in unison with concert pitch.

Here is a rule about transposition of brass instruments which you must memorize and remember always. All brass instruments, when written in the bass clef, (with the exception of the French Horn), are non-transposing instruments; i.e., they play exactly the pitches which are written for them in the bass clef.

All brass instruments, when written in the treble clef; are always transposing instruments.

The E♭ baritone and bass instruments include the E♭ Baritone Saxophone, the E♭ Tuba in treble clef, the E♭ Baritone Sarrusophone; the E♭ Contra-Bass Clarinet; all sound an octave and a major sixth lower than concert pitch "Middle C", and must be written an octave and a major sixth higher than concert pitch to sound in unison. See example below:

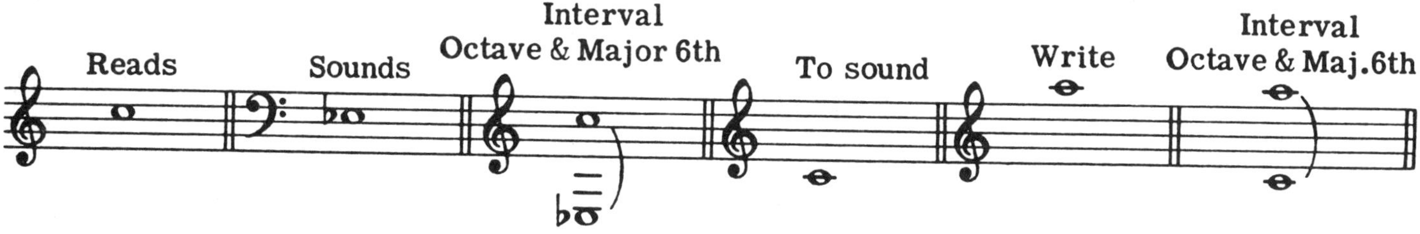

EXERCISE 129. Transpose this melody for E♭ Baritone and Bass instruments to sound in unison with concert pitch. (Note similarity of position on staff after transposing. This is a quick way to transpose. Simply add 3 sharps to key and change clef sign.)

The BB♭ bass instruments, referred to as Double B♭ instruments include the Bass Saxophones, the BB♭ Sousaphone or Tuba in treble clef. These sound two octaves and a major second below the concert pitch, so they must be written two octaves and a major second above the concert pitch. See example below:

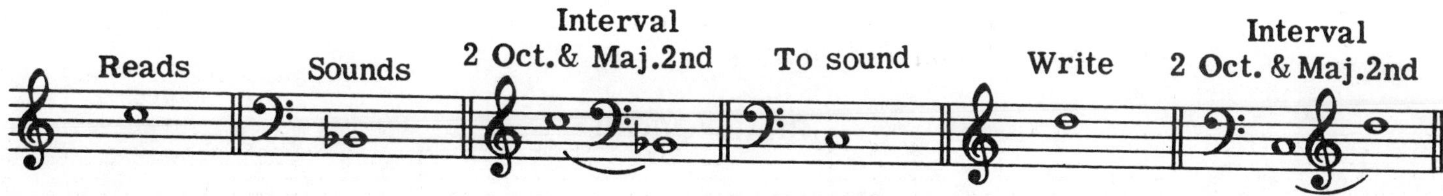

EXERCISE 130. Transpose this melody for BB♭ instruments to sound in unison with concert pitch.

Ranges of Orchestra and Band Instruments

STRING CHOIR

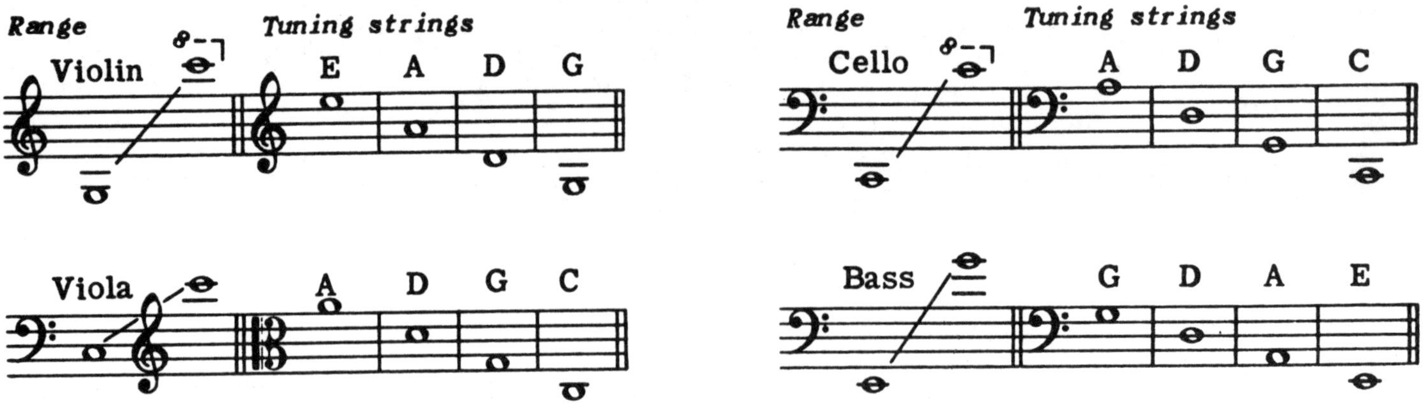

Range *Tuning strings*

Violin 8– E A D G

Range *Tuning strings*

Cello 8– A D G C

Viola A D G C

Bass G D A E

WOODWIND CHOIR

Piccolo 8–

Flute 8–

Clarinet

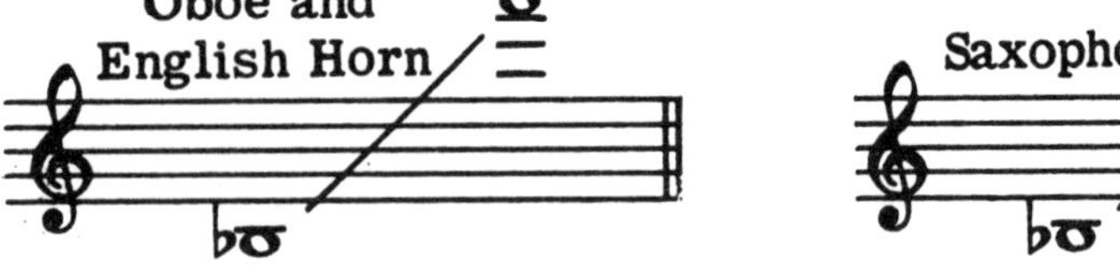

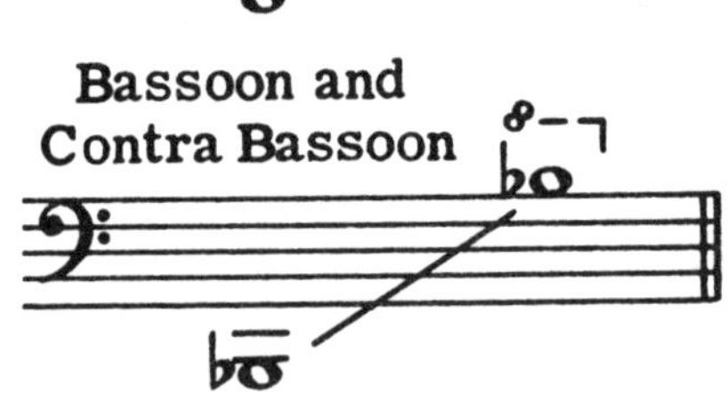

BRASS CHOIR

Simple Orchestration

EXERCISE 131. Arrange this hymn for String Orchestra.

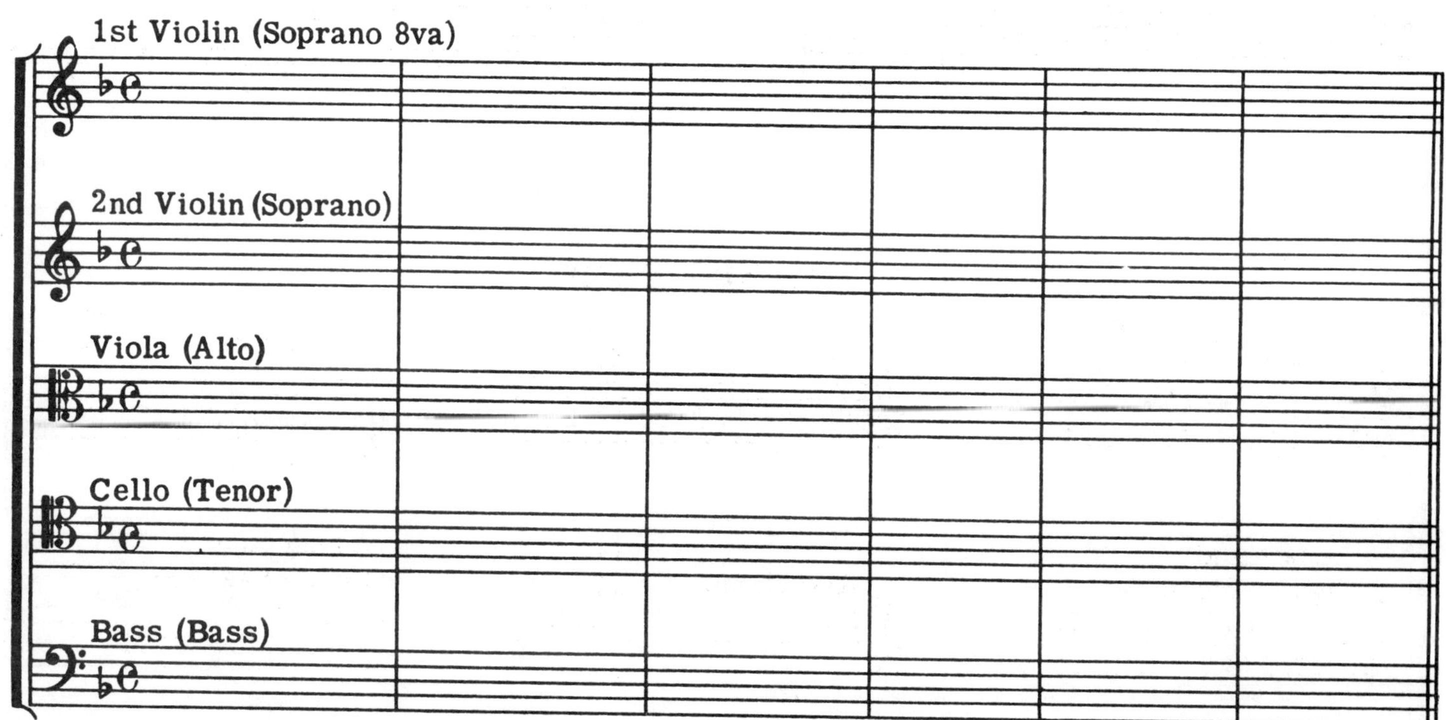

EXERCISE 132. Transpose and arrange this hymn for Brass Choir. Add key signatures.

B♭ Cornet (Soprano)

E♭ Mellophone (Alto)

French Horn in F (Tenor)

Baritone in treble clef (Bass)

EXERCISE 133. Transpose and arrange this hymn for Woodwind choir. Add key signatures.

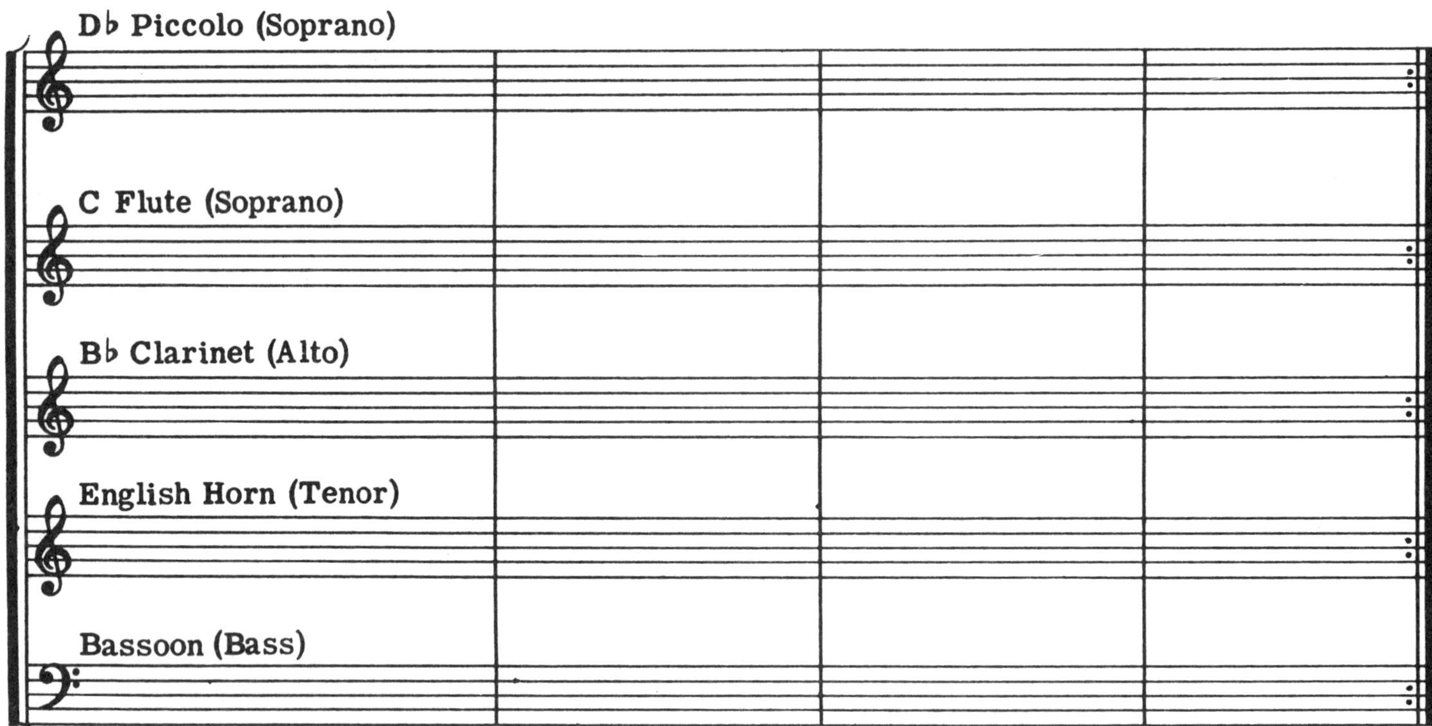

EXERCISE 134. Transpose and arrange this hymn for Saxophone choir. Add key signatures.

B♭ Soprano

E♭ Alto

B♭ Tenor

E♭ Baritone (Bass)

CHAPTER 22
Review

EXERCISE 135. Write one example of each of the following intervals. Minor Third, Major Second, Minor Sixth, Major Seventh, Augmented Fifth.

EXERCISE 136. Name the following intervals.

EXERCISE 137. Write the Perfect Authentic cadence and the Perfect Plagal cadence, in the key of E♭.

EXERCISE 138. Resolve the following Dominant Seventh chords.

EXERCISE 139. Place the symbol over each chord. Also figure the bass. Circle every passing tone.

Abide With Me

EXERCISE 140. Write the three forms of the minor scale on the keynote G.

EXERCISE 141. Place the symbol over each chord. Also figure the bass. Circle every passing tone.

EXERCISE 142. Resolve the following chords.

EXERCISE 143. Copy and harmonize the following melodies as indicated.

Then You'll Remember Me
Bohemian Girl-Balfe
Two part harmony
4
Two part harmony with piano accompaniment.
La Donna Mobile-Rigoletto
5
Three part harmony with piano accompaniment.
Danube Waves
6
Four part harmony.
Home on the Range
7